# Motivate
# People

# Motivate People

Get the best from
yourself and others

**GAVIN INGHAM**

LONDON, NEW YORK,
MUNICH, MELBOURNE, DELHI

Produced for Dorling Kindersley
by **terry jeavons**&**company**

Project Editor                Fiona Biggs
Project Art Editor            Terry Jeavons
Designer                      JC Lanaway

Senior Editor                 Simon Tuite
Editor                        Tom Broder
Senior Art Editor             Sara Robin
DTP Designer                  Traci Salter
Production Controller         Stuart Masheter

Executive Managing Editor     Adèle Hayward
Managing Art Editor           Nick Harris

Art Director                  Peter Luff
Publisher                     Corinne Roberts

Special Photography           Mike Hemsley

First published in 2007 by Dorling Kindersley Limited
80 Strand, London, WC2R 0RL
The Penguin Group
2 4 6 8 10 9 7 5 3 1
Copyright © 2007 Dorling Kindersley Limited
Text copyright © 2007 Gavin Ingham

ED250
Printed and bound in China by Leo Paper Group

# Contents

# Introduction

**Whether you are a team leader, a manager, or co-worker, the ability to motivate people is fundamental to your ability to achieve your business and personal goals. Helping yourself and others to get and stay motivated is an important tool for any successful person.**

What motivates one person will not be what motivates another, and, for this reason, many managers do not have the ability or the skills to build a motivated team. *Motivate People* will help you to unlock strategies and techniques that will allow you to motivate others both in the short and the long term. Aimed primarily at people who work, it will also be an important resource for those who want to know more about their motivation in their life outside work.

> **The best motivators are those who help people to help themselves**

Why is one individual motivated by a certain task when another person isn't? How is it that one person can control emotions better than another? What can you do to remove blocks to personal motivation? By following the advice given here you will discover what's really important to people and will be able to use it to motivate them consistently.

Learn how to set goals that stretch your teams and create and maintain structures that help you to stay on track and keep your teams motivated. Work/life balance, training and development, and personal growth are all important factors. You will need to discover how to attract motivated people into your organization, how to look after them and ensure that they feel valued, and how to reward them, create long-term motivation, and inspire loyalty.

People are more motivated when they feel that they are understood. You need to really understand the people on your teams and to listen for the meaning behind what they are saying. By focusing on core coaching and management skills you will be able to achieve their consistent motivation.

If people understand what causes them to feel motivated and what doesn't they will be encouraged to take responsibility for their own motivation. If you want to motivate yourself or help others to become motivated, this book will be essential reading.

# Self-Assessment

This assessment is designed to get you thinking about how you motivate people, and may lead to new insights. Whether you are an experienced motivator, or just starting out, you will get the most from this assessment if you do it twice, once before you read the book, and again after you have finished the book and, crucially, done the exercises.

Before    After

**1 Why do you get demotivated?**

**A** People and circumstances upset or annoy me.
**B** I am not getting the results that I would like.
**C** I am not taking responsibility for my own motivation.

**2 Why do you think the motivation of your team is not always as high as you would like it be?**

**A** My team members are basically lazy and don't care about their work enough.
**B** Everyone has bad days and it can't be helped.
**C** I haven't taken the time to fully understand them and help them to be more consistently motivated.

**3 How focused are you when you are listening to someone speak?**

**A** I always do at least two things at a time, so I will be writing or sorting papers while I listen.
**B** I listen for as long as is necessary for me to give relevant advice and ideas.
**C** I focus my full attention on the individual with the sole intention of understanding what is being said.

**4 Why do you believe that people should be motivated at work?**

**A** They would get disciplined if they weren't.
**B** That's what you have to do to get on in life.
**C** Work is an opportunity to achieve your personal goals and aspirations.

| | Before | After |
|---|---|---|

**5** **How are mistakes viewed in your business?**

- **A** They are something to be avoided. We don't come to work to make mistakes.
- **B** They are tolerated in junior staff but more experienced people really shouldn't be making mistakes.
- **C** As a learning experience. You can't make progress unless you make a few mistakes.

**6** **What do the members of your team think about feedback?**

- **A** They avoid feedback and become defensive when they are given any.
- **B** They listen politely but rarely act on it.
- **C** They welcome it because it gives them encouragement and guidance and allows them to see how they are progressing.

**7** **What do you base your day-to-day motivational approach upon?**

- **A** How I feel on the day and what sort of approach I think my team deserves.
- **B** The way my boss used to motivate/manage me.
- **C** A considered system of motivation that I have tailored carefully to suit my teams.

**8** **How do you view goal setting?**

- **A** I don't set goals – it's too much effort and I don't think it achieves anything.
- **B** I set some verbal goals for some activities.
- **C** I have well-formed goals, which are written down and which I review regularly.

**9** **How do you go about finding the right people for your teams?**

- **A** I rely mainly on luck and gut instinct.
- **B** It's usuallly a process of trial and error.
- **C** I've put in place a formalized approach to recruitment that ensures consistency of approach and selection.

**10** **What do you think about training and coaching?**

- **A** Training is a waste of time and does not reflect the issues/challenges that my team faces in the real world.
- **B** Training should be done when you have a need or something specific for which people require training, for example a new computer system.
- **C** It's an essential part of staff motivation and should be consistent, regular, and developmental.

|  | | Before | After |
|--|--|--------|-------|

**11** **Why do you hold regular meetings?**

**A** I don't hold regular meetings.
**B** To tell people how they have performed, keep them on the straight and narrow, and give necessary discipline and orders.
**C** To educate, motivate, and inspire; to keep people informed about progress and objectives; to share company news; to allow them to share on the challenges/issues/problems they face; to get them involved through shared ideas and training.

**12** **How do you view staff rewards?**

**A** I don't believe that people should be rewarded for the job they're paid to do.
**B** I think that rewards can be given occasionally to reward exceptional behaviour.
**C** I know what my team members value and I give them regular encouragement through rewards and praise.

**13** **I am the manager of my team because:**

**A** I am the most qualified and I know best.
**B** I have been around longest and I have consistently achieved the best results.
**C** I am good at understanding people and helping them to motivate themselves.

**14** **When things go wrong around here:**

**A** Everyone looks for someone to blame.
**B** We analyze the situation carefully before someone takes responsibility.
**C** We focus on the outcome we want and put our energy into achieving that result.

## Final Scores

|  | A | B | C |
|--|---|---|---|
| **Before** | | | |
| **After** | | | |

# Analysis

## Mostly As

These answers suggest that you don't take responsibility for motivation – either your own or that of others. You generally see yourself as right and don't take the time to understand others. You don't plan or prepare enough for challenges and issues. To change things, follow the advice in the book and do the exercises. Starting with small, achievable steps, you should soon have some evidence of positive results. Use these early successes to encourage yourself to get even better results.

## Mostly Bs

You're probably not a bad motivator. You no doubt get some good results from your team and your B answers are pretty normal. You do, however, feel frustrated at times that the motivational levels in your team are not consistent. As you read the book pay close attention to areas where you think you can benefit most. Do the exercises and think about them in relation to your experiences. What are some key things you can do to achieve more Cs in your next assessment?

## Mostly Cs

You demonstrate a balanced approach to motivation. You take responsibility for your own success and have a good understanding of how to get the best out of others. However, don't become complacent. Read the book carefully, do the exercises, and look for complementary ideas and strategies that will help you to become an even better motivator. The best motivators are always open to learning as they believe that they can always improve.

## Conclusion

If this is the first time that you have done this self-assessment, bear in mind the analysis when you read the book. Pay special attention to the areas highlighted by your responses, as well as the tips and techniques – these will help you to reduce the number of A responses next time and achieve a more balanced mixture of Bs and Cs. After you have completed the book and put the techniques into practice, do the assessment again. Giving honest answers will enable you to get a direct measure of your progress – you should be able to see a big improvement. Most of all have fun with this test. It is a tool to help you develop, not something to browbeat yourself with.

# 1

# How to Be a Motivator

To be a great motivator you need to understand yourself and others. Becoming more aware of why you do what you do and learning to control your emotions will help you to get better results. The techniques in this chapter can be used both on yourself and with the members of your team. You will learn how to:

- Discover what's important to you and others
- Take responsibility for your emotional state
- Direct your mind to become more focused and solution oriented
- Uncover limiting beliefs and create the mindset of a motivator.

# Discover What's Important

Good motivators know what motivates people. If you do not know what people value then you will find that you will not be able to motivate them at all.

## Let Your Values Dictate What is Important

What you value determines what life means to you. When people become detached from their values they become unmotivated. Because of a general lack of awareness of what is important, detachment and demotivation are very common. For example many people watch a great deal of television every day, but this is unlikely to be because they consider the programmes they watch to be high priorities. Helping people to get reconnected and properly aligned with their own values is a powerful management tool.

## Identify what Motivates People

It is always a mistake to assume that what is important to you is important to others. Many managers try to motivate people with promises of financial reward and promotion. This may be because these are the factors that motivate the managers. When asked, few staff place these two motivators at the top of their lists, preferring instead more intangible motivators such as feeling valued and being listened to.

**Find the Motivators**
People who do the same job or who have the same interests may have very different motivators. It is up to you to discover what these motivators are.

# think
## SMART

**One of the most powerful motivational activities is keeping your own log book. Most successful people keep a written record of what they do.**

A log book will help you to capture thoughts and aspirations, record successes and key learning points, and outline your goals and ambitions. You will be able to monitor your progress and assess how successfully you are running your life.

## What Motivates You?

Spend a few minutes thinking about your life so far. Think about some of the activities that really excited you at different stages in your life and development. These should be things that really mattered to you at the time and gave you a great sense of satisfaction. Make a list of these activities and then answer the following questions:

- Which of these activities has given you the greatest sense of satisfaction?
- What abilities or skills do you most like using?
- Why do you like using these abilities and skills so much?
- What patterns do you notice in your list of things that mattered to you?

Now describe yourself when you engaged in these activities.

- What do you see, hear, feel, and think? Describe what you are doing, who you're with, and the way in which people respond to you. The more you do this exercise the more powerful it will become.

## 5 minute FIX

**Establish what really motivates you in different areas.**

- Take one area (work) and ask, "What is important to me about (work)?"

- Write a one-line response to this: "I want to be recognized for my contribution to the team."

# Know Your Values

**If you are living a balanced life you will be able to give sufficient attention to every area. Learning to balance your priorities will help you to motivate yourself and the members of your team.**

## Determine Your Priorities

Before you can work on balancing priorities it is important that you understand what those priorities are. Examine the diagram on the facing page and write each of the eight areas of the wheel of life on to separate stick-on notes. Consider each area in turn and decide which one is least important. Throw away the note that has that area written on it. Continue to discard those areas that are least important until only two notes remain. Which two areas of your life remain? Most people have one or both of Loving Relationships and Health and Fitness. Very few people retain either Money or Work.

Sometimes the most obvious motivators are not what inspire people to act. As a motivator you need to be aware of this and discover people's real motivators – if you fail to motivate the whole person you will fail as a motivator.

# Case study: Living Up to Your Own Values

Claire, a recently promoted under-performing sales manager, was constantly stressed and under pressure. She was failing to hit targets and her work problems were beginning to affect her relationship with her partner. After working on the Wheel of Life she decided to move back into a senior sales role and quickly regained her motivation and sense of purpose.

• *By understanding what was important to her Claire realized that she had sought promotion to make her family and friends proud of her.*
• *She learned that she preferred the challenge and focus of her old sales role.*
• *By moving back into her old job she was able to feel fulfilled and her values were met.*

## Use the Wheel Of Life

By visualizing your values as a wheel you can see the impact of an imbalance on your sense of self and, consequently, your motivation.

→ **Health and fitness** Your physical energy and vitality

→ **Wellbeing** Your personal sense of peace

→ **Career/Work** Your day-to-day occupation

→ **Finance** Your salary/savings/investments

→ **Family** Your immediate family and other relatives

→ **Loving relationships** Your friends and partner

→ **Social** Relaxation/pastimes/hobbies

→ **Personal development/Growth** Self-improvement

Give yourself a score from 1–10 for each area of your life, where 1 = least amount of fulfilment and 10 = most amount of fulfilment.

Reflect on your wheel. What areas do you need to work on? What do you want the wheel to look like in a year, in five years, and in ten years?

# Learn to Motivate Yourself

**Motivation is about having the right attitude at the
right time. It enables you to access your skills and
perform the task in hand effectively and efficiently.**

## Control Your Emotions

Good motivators teach the members of their team how to
be more aware of their attitudes and how to control them.
This in turn has an impact on the behaviours that these
people exhibit. In order to teach others how to control
their emotions you must be able to control your own.

## Access Your Personal Motivation

Most people view motivation as something that is
determined by external events and circumstances and is
out of their control. They are motivated from the outside
in. If you feel demotivated and lack confidence you are
unlikely to make a good presentation, whereas if you are
confident and motivated you will probably make an
excellent one. A poor presentation will affect the way you
feel about yourself and will determine your subsequent
behaviour, increasing the likelihood of another poor result.

## think SMART

**While skills are essential for success, unless the
people on your team are in the right state of mind,
they will not be able to access their skills effectively.**

List ten attributes, such as confidence and focus, that the
members of your team display collectively on a day when
everything is going well. Most teams produce a list that is
more about attitudes than skills. Whenever they are having a
bad day and are feeling unmotivated, encourage them by
showing them their list of attributes and reminding them of
just how good they are.

## Know Your Motivators

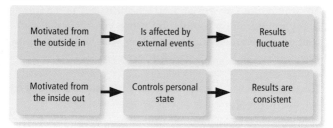

## Motivate Yourself from the Inside Out

Top performers know that their mental state or motivation is an internal representation of how they view things. To be a good motivator you need to understand how to motivate yourself, regardless of external circumstances, and you must then teach your teams how to do this too.

**Check the Motivators**
When you analyze someone's performance, it is important to know whether that person is motivated from the inside out or the outside in, as this will affect their results.

## Watch Their Language

People often give an indication as to whether they take responsibility for their own motivation or allow themselves to be affected by external events. This will be evident in their response to events – self-motivated people will talk about what they can do to improve a situation, while those affected by external events will blame those events.

### Positive Responses to External Events

**HIGH IMPACT**

- I was angry
- I need to learn from this
- How can I motivate myself?
- I need to prioritize my workload
- We need to create a positive working environment

**NEGATIVE IMPACT**

- It annoyed me
- It's not my fault
- The weather's getting me down
- It's all getting on top of me
- The working environment here is very demotivating

# Change Your Internal State

Becoming more aware of your emotions in the moment is key to improving motivation. Once you have realized that your attitude is not supporting you, you need to be able to change it quickly and effectively.

## Change Your Physiology to Change Your State

When you meet someone you can usually tell how he is feeling even before he tells you. This is because you unconsciously notice his physiology. Your physiology is your physical being: the way you stand, sit, move, breathe, and so on. Every emotional state has a certain physiology attached to it. Someone who is depressed would have a very different physiology from someone who is motivated. He would probably be slouching, breathing slowly, looking down – and he certainly wouldn't be smiling. Someone who is motivated would be sitting up straight, breathing energetically, with his eyes focused and his head up – and he would probably be smiling. You can change your physiology by controlling your posture, changing your expression, or altering your breathing. This will enable you to change your mental state almost instantly.

## TECHNIQUES *to* practise

If you are feeling demotivated, this will affect not only your work but also the motivation of your team.

Whenever this happens you will have to act quickly to increase your motivation – use this technique when the need arises.

- Stand up and take a few slow, deep breaths.
- Hold up your head and pull back your shoulders.
- Think of a time when you were really motivated and imagine yourself in that motivated state.
- Make this picture of yourself brighter and more defined.
- Step into the picture and allow yourself to experience a feeling of total motivation.

## Change Your Mental Focus

Mental focus is the general term used to describe a person's thought processes. These processes fit into two general areas – your self-talk

**Improve Your Focus**
Learning to focus while performing any activity will train you to access a state of motivation.

and the mental images that you are constantly forming in your head. The combination of these two, along with your particular physiology, will determine your mental state at any given time.

## Talk to Yourself

When any event or situation occurs you form a mental picture of the event (and maybe the outcome) in your head. You talk to yourself (in your head!) about the event and your feelings about it. Two people in the same situation will create entirely different representations of the same event, which means that their experience of the event is not the same. By taking control of your pictures and your self-talk you can master your own motivation.

# Focus Your Mind

**The power to focus is a rare skill. By developing your ability to focus you will be able to improve your motivation, your productivity, and your creativity.**

## Use Your Focus to Stay Motivated

Focus is defined both as the centre of interest or activity and a state of clear definition. People who have clarity of focus know what they want and are able to remain motivated regardless of external events or circumstances. Everyone is capable of focusing perfectly. The problem is not so much an inability to focus, more an inability to focus on what you want. By taking control of your mental focus you will get more of the results that you want. By helping others to focus you can improve their results, their morale, and, ultimately, their productivity.

## Seven-Day Mental Focus Plan

If you stop to think about it, you will probably notice how often your focus strays. Over a period of seven days, concentrate on raising your habitual levels of focus. Before you start to work on any important task, ask yourself:

→ What do I need to be focusing on?
→ How can I really focus on this task?
→ Why is it important to me that I stay focused on this task?

When you have completed the seven days, assess your ability to focus. Notice how much better at focusing you have become. Imagine what you could achieve in three months if you were to use this strategy consistently. What would this mean for your relationships, for your motivational abilities, and for the success of your organization?

## Get Focused

| Needs Work! | Average | Good |
|---|---|---|
| I struggle to focus | I sometimes lose focus | I am always 100 per cent focused |
| I frequently get distracted | I occasionally get distracted | I never lose my focus |
| I think I am unfocused | I have average levels of focus | I am a very focused person |
| Other people say that I am easily distracted | Other people say that I have normal levels of focus | Other people say that I am very focused |
| I never start things when I say I will and I don't keep to schedules | I miss some schedules but meet others | I start tasks on time and keep to my schedules |
| I cannot focus myself consciously | I can focus myself if I try really hard | I know how to get focused and have strategies for staying focused |

## Improve Your Focus

Achieving clarity of focus will usually require a good deal of practice. You should try to work consciously on improving clarity of focus when you are engaged in tasks that don't always hold your interest. For example, if you find that the administrative aspect of your job fails to hold your attention, try to clear your mind of other matters and focus on the importance of what you are doing. Check yourself periodically to establish if, and to what extent, your ability to focus has improved – are there still some areas that need a bit more work?

**Test Your Focus**
Look at these statements and rate yourself by circling the answer that best matches your situation. If you have any areas that "need work" or are simply "average" you have a good opportunity to improve your focus.

## Focus on Success

By learning to focus on the solutions that you want you will achieve better results. Good motivators focus on getting the results that they want. They then choose an appropriate action that will maximize the possibility of achieving them.

A change of focus often gets a better result

## Act – Don't React

Most people spend most of their time and energy thinking about and acting upon problems, challenges, and issues – they react to situations. By constantly focusing on problems they compound the original difficulty and reinforce its negative effects. If you learn to change your focus so that you are concentrating on the positive outcome of whatever activity you are engaged in you will soon find that you are actually achieving the results that you want.

## Case study: Being Motivated to Change

Mary, a sales manager, held regular team meetings but people would turn up late and slouch in their chairs looking uninterested. She was soon expecting this behaviour even before she started the meetings and her approach gradually became defensive and authoritarian. Her team did not respond to this and the meetings became steadily more unproductive.

Mary realized that she would have to do something to overcome this problem and she arranged a coaching session for herself. This helped her to change her behaviour and run effective motivational meetings with the full involvement of her team.

• The coaching helped Mary to focus on and visualize the format, content, and results of the meetings.
• Because she began to take responsibility for the success of the meetings they soon became more productive.

## The Six Steps to Success

**When motivating individuals you will always encounter challenges and problems. Your focus will determine the way you act and the results that you get in these situations. This six-step strategy will help you to focus on success.**

**1** Acknowledge the event. The first step to getting the results we want is to acknowledge that there has been a problem.

**2** Consider your current response or reaction to the event. How do you think and feel about this event or challenge?

**3** What is the normal outcome of this situation? This is usually very easy to predict, as the same actions repeated in response to a similar event or situation will usually bring about similar results.

**4** What are the consequences of these results for you? What do they mean for your motivation? What do they mean for the motivation of your team? What will the consequences be for your organization?

**5** What results would you like to achieve? You cannot do anything about an event that has already happened, but you can focus on a different outcome to a similar event.

**6** Plan your actions so that they drive you in the direction of the outcome that you want. Choose carefully and take some time to visualize yourself responding to a similar event in the future with your new, more resourceful actions, and getting your desired results.

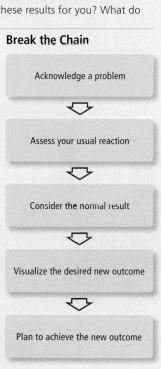

**Break the Chain**

Acknowledge a problem

⬇

Assess your usual reaction

⬇

Consider the normal result

⬇

Visualize the desired new outcome

⬇

Plan to achieve the new outcome

# Challenge Your Beliefs

Having the right mindset is essential to being a good motivator. Whether you have a fully supportive mindset will depend on your established beliefs about your current situation.

## Believe in Yourself

If a member of your team is feeling unmotivated it may be because of what he believes. Beliefs drive the way a person feels and, therefore, the way he behaves, yet few people are aware of the impact that their beliefs can have on their lives. Even fewer consciously choose their beliefs. Beliefs come from many different sources: family, history, friends, colleagues, culture, politics, education, training, managers, experience, religion, media, television, the Internet. Even if what you believe isn't true, that belief will still affect your life. The belief that your lack of success can be attributed to the way your parents brought you up may or may not be true, but it could keep you from achieving the success that you want.

**Trust Yourself** A truly empowering belief may be a certainty that you grew up with, and will be a strong motivator, giving you real confidence in what you do.

## Empower Yourself

Motivators must be able to distinguish between limiting beliefs and empowering beliefs. Limiting beliefs are those beliefs that cause you to feel unresourceful in a situation. Empowering beliefs are those beliefs that cause you to feel resourceful in the same situation. If you fail to identify and help others to remove limiting beliefs, these beliefs will reinforce themselves and become self-fulfilling.

## Acknowledge Limiting Beliefs

Limiting beliefs are the result of limiting decisions made at some point in the past, often in early childhood before you had fully developed the ability to make sense of what was happening in your life. If you were to review these past events with your adult resources and logical abilities you would probably come to quite different conclusions. It is important to acknowledge limiting beliefs, whatever their source, because you can then take whatever further learning you need from them and let them go.

**Beliefs drive the way a person feels and behaves**

## Reinforce Your Beliefs

To help you to eradicate any limiting beliefs that you may have, try viewing them from a different perspective. You can do this by asking yourself the following questions:

- Is this belief true?
- Has there ever been a time when it wasn't true?
- Would someone else believe it to be true?
- What evidence challenges this belief?
- What is it costing me to believe this?
- How will I benefit from letting this belief go now?

---

**TIP** **When someone feels unresourceful try to find out which of his beliefs makes him feel like that.**

---

# Create a Motivational Mindset

**Developing a positive belief system for yourself is key to being able to motivate others. Think of someone who has motivated you in the past and ask yourself what his beliefs were and how they motivated him.**

## Look to the Great Motivators

Great motivators help others to identify and build on positive evidential references that will support empowering beliefs. Highly motivated teams share references and evidence of their joint and individual successes, thus building mutually supportive beliefs. If you were a great motivator what would you believe about your team members, your organization, your resources, your identity, your ability to motivate? Great motivators know that individuals have untapped potential and that they can be more motivated and achieve more than they ever thought possible. Take responsibility for your own beliefs and stay focused on references that support your aims and goals.

# Case study: Changing Your Approach

Davina had recently taken over a new team. One of the team members, Josh, was described as a lazy under-achiever. Davina soon noted Josh's poor performance and became annoyed, excluding Josh from important projects.

After speaking with her own coach about this issue, Davina sought coaching for Josh. The coaching revealed that Josh believed that no-one noticed or believed in him. He always felt unappreciated and worthless.

Davina decided to change her approach to Josh, who began to perform more effectively and with renewed energy and self-esteem.

• *The coaching process showed that Davina had failed to recognize Josh's good points because of the preconceptions that she had inherited about him.*
• *Davina's willingness to revise her attitude gave Josh the opportunity to perform as a valuable team member.*

## Reinforce Your Beliefs

When faced with challenges and problems, having a supportive belief system will help you to remain focused and motivated. If you are to be able to turn good ideas into empowering beliefs you may need to do some work on them.

**Be Inspiring** Try to emulate a good role model. You will be an inspiring leader if you yourself can take your inspiration from someone whose qualities and performance you admire.

- Think of a situation that you find yourself in where you sometimes feel unmotivated.
- Ask yourself, "What do I need to believe about myself/ this situation so that I can feel totally motivated?"
- Write down up to five of these beliefs in your logbook. Post them on your computer.
- Find evidence to support each of your new beliefs. Ask yourself, "What evidence supports this belief?"
- Focus at least once a day on your new beliefs and the evidence that supports them.

# Summary: Believing to Achieve

To be a really good motivator you need to understand what motivates others. First of all, though, you need to become aware of what your own personal motivators are. Learn to focus on what you want, acknowledging any limiting beliefs that may be holding you back from achieving what you want in life.

## Believing in Yourself

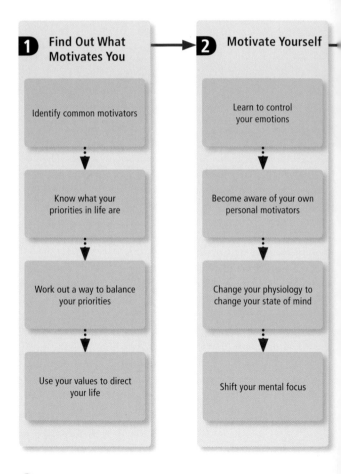

**1** Find Out What Motivates You

Identify common motivators

Know what your priorities in life are

Work out a way to balance your priorities

Use your values to direct your life

**2** Motivate Yourself

Learn to control your emotions

Become aware of your own personal motivators

Change your physiology to change your state of mind

Shift your mental focus

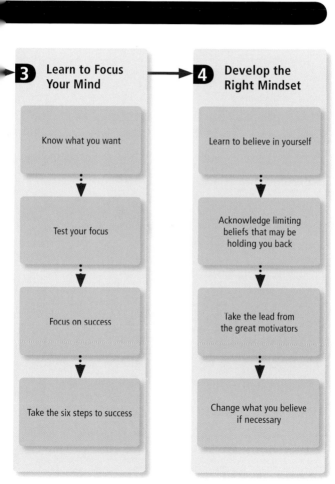

**3** **Learn to Focus Your Mind** → **4** **Develop the Right Mindset**

| Learn to Focus Your Mind | Develop the Right Mindset |
|---|---|
| Know what you want | Learn to believe in yourself |
| Test your focus | Acknowledge limiting beliefs that may be holding you back |
| Focus on success | Take the lead from the great motivators |
| Take the six steps to success | Change what you believe if necessary |

# Structure 2
# Success

By studying motivational theories you can set yourself up for success, but obstacles will sometimes get in the way. You need to learn how to set goals, deal with resistance, and implement structures that will help you to achieve the motivational success that you need. This chapter explains how to:

- Apply the motivational theories of Maslow, Herzberg, Likert, and Vroom
- Get leverage for the motivational change that lies ahead
- Set goals that motivate, inspire, and stretch
- Design and implement structures that support your goals.

# Maslow's Hierarchy of Needs

**Many interesting theories of motivation have been developed over the years. One of them is psychologist Abraham Maslow's Hierarchy of Needs, which is useful when working with individuals and teams.**

## Meet Lower Level Needs First

Maslow believed that people progress up the hierarchy of needs, starting with meeting physiological needs and ending with self-actualization. Once a need is met you will no longer be motivated by this need and will move on to the next motivator. Conversely, you will not be motivated by higher level needs until the lower ones are met.

- **Physiological needs** – Having sufficient water, food, warmth, sex, exercise, and sleep.
- **Security requirements** – Being safe from the dangers and difficulties of life. Not having to worry about survival risks such as accidents, attack, droughts, and ill health. Having security of employment and finance.
- **Social needs and belonging** – Being close to those around you. Wanting to be well liked by them. People like to belong to groups – family, social, and geographic groups.
- **Esteem and personal status** – Having a good social standing in the perception of others. Needing to be well liked, highly regarded, and appreciated.
- **Self-actualization** – Being the best that you can be and releasing your individual potential purely for your own personal satisfaction.

### Maslow's Hierarchy

SELF-ACTUALIZATION

ESTEEM AND PERSONAL STATUS

SOCIAL NEEDS

SECURITY

PHYSIOLOGICAL NEEDS

## Be a Positive Motivator

**HIGH IMPACT**

- Encouraging personal development and growth
- Teaching communication and confidence techniques
- Fostering team spirit
- Demonstrating organizational stability and loyalty
- Meeting people's physical needs in the workplace

**NEGATIVE IMPACT**

- Ignoring individual's development possibilities
- Pushing people into situations for which they are not prepared
- Ignoring team dynamics
- Hiring and firing at will instead of instituting proper procedures
- Cutting down on necessities to save money

## Be Creative

Many managers use money to motivate people, through commission structures and bonus schemes. However, if your monetary needs are met and you do not link extra money to the achievement of any higher needs, then it is unlikely that money alone will motivate you effectively. You may decide that the extra money is not worth the increased effort required. In these circumstances a manager who wants to motivate you will need to be creative and focus on your higher level needs.

## Use the Hierarchy of Needs

You can understand a lot about a person by identifying her current position in Maslow's Hierarchy. Try thinking about your team members, your friends, and your colleagues. How do you think their position in the hierarchy affects their motivation when carrying out day-to-day tasks? How do you think you could you use this knowledge to help them to become more motivated?

**TIP** When working with teams, weigh up the needs of the individual in relation to the team, and tie the individual's motivating factors into those of the team.

# Use the Motivational Theories

Other theories that will make it easier for you to learn how to motivate include Frederick Herzberg's Dual Factor Theory, Rensis Likert's Sales Management Theory, and Victor Vroom's Expectancy Theory.

## The Dual Factor Theory

This theory separates "hygiene" and "motivational" factors. The hygiene factors, which Herzberg considered as necessary but not motivational, include physical working conditions, security, interpersonal relationships, salary and benefits, company procedures, status, and personal circumstances. The motivational factors, which directly motivate people to achieve more, include achievement, recognition, interest value, and responsibility.

## The Sales Management Theories

Likert focused on the link between the behaviour of sales managers and that of their teams, discovering that:

- High-performing sales teams invariably had managers who set themselves high performance goals.
- Managers who encouraged group involvement and discussion in meetings achieved far better results from their teams than those who controlled and dominated.

## The Expectancy Theory

Vroom showed that motivation depends on whether people think their efforts are likely to achieve success or not, using three criteria.

**1 Expectancy** – The extent to which you think increased effort will result in increased performance.

**2 Instrumentality** – How much you think that this increased performance will result in increased reward.

**3 Valence** – How greatly you value the increased reward.

---

**TIP** Encourage people to understand the links between effort, results, and personal benefits.

---

It is important to encourage people to understand the links between effort and results and to show them clearly how they will benefit from the results. They will be better motivated to work at their optimum levels if:
- They think that increasing their efforts will result in improved performance
- They think that they will be rewarded for the extra effort they put in to achieve that performance
- They value that reward.

The theory demonstrates the importance of knowing what is and is not important to every member of your team. It also highlights the conscious choices that people will make in achieving their objective of maximizing pleasure and avoiding pain. Helping the members of your team to link pleasure to important tasks will result in their increased motivation and improved performance.

## Motivate Your Team

Take the lead from the great motivational thinkers and follow these guidelines to ensure that your team is well motivated.

→ Look after the physical comfort of your team in the workplace and ensure that hygiene factors are covered.

→ Reduce worries about job security and market vulnerability.

→ Understand people's individual motivators and their importance in getting the best out of your team.

→ Encourage the members of your team to see the link between their efforts and the results they achieve. Make sure that you clearly link results and reward.

→ Create opportunities for personal, professional, and spiritual advancement, while, at the same time, encouraging people to take responsibility for their own success.

→ Use inter-team meetings to encourage group belonging and foster improved team spirit.

# Achieve High Performance

**The ability to learn, to understand, and to utilize new information, strategies, and behaviours is essential for creating and sustaining motivation.**

## Step Your Way to Success

Whenever you learn anything new you progress through five steps. Sometimes this progression happens so quickly you may be unaware of the process. At other times you will be much more aware of the process and your own feelings surrounding it. Understanding the steps will allow you to understand and motivate people more effectively. There may seem to be an artificial barrier at step 2 conscious incompetence. Make sure that before implementing any new skill, strategy, or behaviour you do a quick motivation "health check", working out how congruent you are with wanting to achieve this goal.

## Case study: Learning to Advance

Seventeen-year-old Maya was keen to learn to drive but was totally unaware of how difficult this was actually going to be (unconscious incompetence). Easing into the driver's seat she grasped the wheel, started the engine, depressed the clutch, put her foot on the accelerator, and stalled the car.

Gradually, Maya realized that learning to drive was going to be a difficult and challenging (conscious incompetence) task. After putting in a lot of practice and effort she eventually reached the point where, if she could maintain her concentration, she was actually able to drive quite proficiently (conscious competence). Maya passed her test and is now a confident driver.

• *By persisting in the face of challenges and difficulties Maya was able to learn the new habits necessary for driving.*
• *She sometimes arrives at her destination and doesn't remember the details of driving there (unconscious competence).*
• *If she focuses on advancing her driving skills she will be able to pursue the state of mastery of the driving process.*

## Five Steps to High Performance

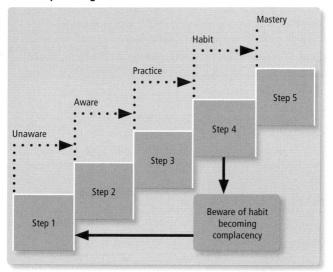

Mastery

Habit

Practice

Aware

Unaware

Step 5

Step 4

Step 3

Step 2

Step 1

Beware of habit becoming complacency

It is important to be aware that people will progress through the five steps at different speeds – everyone's journey towards the state of mastery will be different.

**Achieve Mastery**
If you are to achieve your optimum performance you will have to advance through these five steps.

- **Step 1: Unconscious Incompetence** – You are unaware of what you don't know.
- **Step 2: Conscious Incompetence** – You become aware of what you don't know. You're ignorant and you are aware of your ignorance.
- **Step 3: Conscious Competence** – You become aware of how to do things properly. You have the ability to do something but you have to concentrate on it.
- **Step 4: Unconscious Competence** – You are unaware of how you do the things you know how to do. You do things without even thinking about it.
- **Step 5: Mastery** – This takes you a stage further than unconscious competence – the state of mastery has an additional, almost mystical quality.

## Break Bad Habits

People spend a lot of time operating in an unconscious state, repeating the same mistakes and weaknesses. If your team's current habits and behaviours don't support your objectives then you need to be able to break them. Operating out of habit has many advantages. You can:

- Multitask
- Operate fluidly and easily
- Stay within your comfort zone
- Remain stress free.

However, reacting in a certain way to a certain stimulus may be right in one situation but wrong in another. The key here is to step back periodically and check that your behaviours are getting you the results you want.

## Learn Continually

When you are learning a new skill or behaviour and you reach conscious incompetence, you may experience feelings of stress, frustration, challenge, pain, lack of control, discomfort, fear, and uncertainty. You can change your habitual behaviour by breaking through this barrier. What is required to do this is determination, persistence and repeated practice of the new habit.

## think SMART

**The ability to change your behaviours rapidly is essential when motivating people. However, most things worth learning will feel challenging at first.**

Concentrate on becoming more aware of your habitual behaviours, emotions, and responses to people and situations. Decide how you can change these. Practise, practise, practise, and commit yourself to the change for a predefined period of time. Use these techniques in the workplace or at home to get more of the results that you want.

## Assess Your Habits

The HABIT model (Gavin Ingham 2002) can be used with team members to help them to understand and change their underlying habits and behaviours.

### → Habitual behaviours

What behaviours/habits/emotions do you exhibit? When do you exhibit them? How motivated are you?

### → Ask questions

How do these habits contribute to your day-to-day motivation levels? Do these habits support you or limit you? Do they help or hinder you? Do they create results or failure?

### → Break the habit

If a habitual behaviour doesn't support you, how can you stop doing it right now? What is it costing you to behave in this way? How will you benefit from changing that behaviour now?

### → Install new habits

Decide what the most appropriate habit would be and commit to it for a period of time.

### → Test the new habit

Take the new habit for a test run and try it out, constantly refining and retuning it until you are satisfied.

| | |
|---|---|
| **H** | Habitual behaviours |
| | ▽ |
| **A** | Ask questions |
| | ▽ |
| **B** | Break the habit |
| | ▽ |
| **I** | Install new habits |
| | ▽ |
| **T** | Test the new habit |

---

**TIP** Visualize yourself successfully completing the change – this will be a powerful technique for keeping you on track when breaking long-standing habits.

---

# What Makes People Tick?

It can be difficult to understand why two people doing the same job, for the same pay, and in the same environment will perform so differently, but not everyone is motivated by the same values, ambitions, and challenges. Understanding motivating factors will help you to adapt your approach to specific team members. Common motivators include: Personal development, career advancement, sociability, family, financial reward, lifestyle, security, and novelty.

### Personal Development
People who are driven by a need for personal development enjoy work that they perceive to be stretching, and which allows them to acquire new skills. They may be very motivated by training opportunities and feel disenchanted with their job if they believe that they are not learning anything new.

### Career Advancement
Likely to be quite ambitious, career-orientated people are enthusiastic about roles that will benefit their career, but may neglect work that they don't think will bring them recognition.

### Sociability
Many people enjoy interacting with co-workers and clients. These people quickly establish working relationships and thrive on working in teams, but may not work so well in solo roles.

**Mastery is the state that top performers in all spheres strive for and regularly achieve.** As a motivator you may find this exercise useful when working with individuals, or you can do it yourself to reach an understanding of what motivates you. Ask yourself:

- What will it be like when you achieve a state of mastery? What will you be doing/feeling/thinking? Who will be with you? When will this state be useful to you?
- What do you think you need to learn that will help you to move towards that state of mastery right now?

## Build Your Personal Desire

Many people are constantly in pursuit of that elusive extra edge of performance, that key that will unlock their super motivation. Finding the right focus is essential if you are to achieve sustainable motivation in the long term. The key to lasting persistence, determination, and self-belief is personal desire. When you can attach a strong personal meaning to change, you don't need to remind yourself to be motivated or persistent – it happens automatically as you pursue your goals and ambitions.

## Be Clear About Your Reasons

Successful leaders and motivators know why change is important to their staff and they help them to be clear about these reasons. Uncovering their own personal reasons for change is fundamental to helping people to motivate themselves. Different people will have different reasons for doing things and you must understand these fully if you are to help all the members of your team to be consistently motivated. If people are to change they need to be ready, willing, and able to do so. They need to recognize the importance of changing and to have a strong belief in their ability to do so.

# The Structure of Success

**Success has structure. People work best in environments where they know what is going to happen, when it is going to happen, and with whom it is going to happen.**

## Plan Ahead

Teams and individuals work best when they know what to do. Without a proper structure, managers spend too much time dealing with problems and challenges and too little focusing their energies on leading and motivating. If a manager is always attending to the detail, how will the team know what to do and how to react if an unexpected situation arises when the manager is not present? If the team knows how the manager would deal with a situation, because she has established a proper structure within which to operate, the team members will be more proactive and productive, the organization will benefit in the long term, and the manager's reputation will be enhanced.

# Case study: Predefining Activity

Sarah runs a small business with eight team members. They all know what to do but take their daily direction from Sarah. She visits her important clients regularly but when she leaves the office the team often under-perform, not completing their activities to the same standard as when she is in the office. Sarah realized that she had no system in place that the team could use for guidance when she was out of the office. After she had discussed in detail how things should progress in her absence, the staff took more responsibility for their own success and Sarah was able to continue with her client visits without worrying that her staff would feel unmotivated.

• *By creating systems that the team could follow Sarah was able to outline her expectations clearly.*
• *Once the team knew what to do, and when and how to do it, they were not continually looking to her for direction.*
• *Confidence in the systems allowed Sarah's staff to make decisions and operate effectively in her absence.*

## Clarify Expectations and Objectives

When people are clear about what is expected of them, they will take more responsibility for their own behaviour. Organizational procedures should be fixed and everyone should know what they should be doing, and when.

→ **Promotion** should be clear, transparent, consistent, and linked to activity/performance. Many businesses promote using non-tangible, subjective criteria. These are difficult to justify and can cause widespread motivation issues.

→ **Meetings** should be regular and have consistent structure. The "feeling" should always be the same.

→ **Goals/objectives** should be made clear to the team and it should know that these are going to be achieved.

→ **Coaching and training** are critical to success but only if they are consistent. Many organizations invest in development only when they have problems. This pattern of behaviour will quickly establish a link between training and problems.

→ **Management styles and agendas** should be thought through and fixed. People should always know what to expect from their managers. This knowledge will build up their trust and rapport.

→ **Paperwork and administrative tasks** should be clearly defined. People need to know exactly what they have to do, have sufficient training to do it, and have available support and guidance.

**Transparency and consistency are basic to good management**

→ **Discipline** should always be even-handed, appropriate, and visible.

→ **Environmental issues** such as seating, lighting, desks, windows, phones, and laptop computers may not be true motivators, but perceived unfairness in these areas can give rise to major motivational challenges.

## Motivate Your Team

The ability to "see" how effectively people are operating at different logical levels will help you to intervene successfully. Look at how people are working and you will be able to recognize the logical levels in action. Ask yourself:

→ What results do you want to get in your business?
→ What environment would support this?

Think about the behaviours you would like to see people displaying consistently in order to achieve the results you need. Analyze the capabilities they would need to do this. How would they feel about their situation? What emotions would they display? Ask yourself what beliefs they hold that would support their feelings and behaviours. Find out what is important to them and what their image of themselves is.

## Understand the Logical Levels

Logical levels help you to recognize and understand patterns and structures within your business, clarify where problems originate, and give you the necessary insight to correct the problem.

- **Environment** – The physical environment and the people around you
- **Results** – The results that you get
- **Behaviour** – Your activities and behaviours
- **Capabilities** – What you are capable of doing. The sum of your knowledge, skills, and processes
- **Attitudes and emotions** – How you feel about your current situation
- **Beliefs** – What you believe about your situation
- **Values** – What is important to you
- **Identity** – The person you believe yourself to be. Your own personal identity.

## Align the Logical Levels

When trying to elicit change most managers intervene at the behavioural level ("work harder") and occasionally at the capability level (training). To create sustainable change you need to ensure that a person's attitudes, beliefs, values, and identity are aligned in order to support the required change. If these are not in place, motivation will be short-lived.

## Address Values and Beliefs

Helping someone to discover that nurturing and motivating a team of people can produce far better results than focusing purely on the activity of that team is a powerful aim. Provide evidence and references for team leaders so that they can change their belief to one that focuses on developing the team's abilities.

**Create the Right Environment** Working in a well-planned and pleasant working environment can help to increase motivation.

# Set the Right Goals

It is essential that you encourage people to set their own goals and targets. Goals provide both direction and motivation and act as support on days when things are not going exactly the way you want them to.

## Know What You Want

What motivates one person may not motivate another. Some individuals are motivated by one big goal whereas others need smaller, mini-goals. You need to encourage people to set goals for the short term (daily/weekly), medium term (monthly/yearly), and long term (decades/ lifetimes). Many people fail to set or focus upon goals. This can result in a lack of direction and in low motivation. Common reasons for failing to set goals include lack of know-how, laziness, fear of failure, and lack of focus. Goal setting is critical for maintaining motivation and should always be congruent with your values and beliefs.

**Goals must be specific, realistic, and stretching**

## Set Goals that Work

When working with others ask these ten questions to ensure that their goals will be motivational and effective.

- What exactly do you want?
- Where are you at the moment in relation to this goal?
- How will you know when you achieve it?
- What will you see/hear/feel/smell/taste when you achieve this goal?
- Why is this so important to you?
- What will achieving it do for you?
- Where, when, how, and with whom do you want to achieve the goal?
- What resources do you need to achieve this outcome?
- What will be different as a result of achieving the goal?
- Do you believe that you can achieve this goal?

## Achieve Your Goals

**Using imagery is an important part of successful goal setting. By clearly visualizing, your brain will be able to "experience" the achievement of your goals prior to your having achieved them. Repeat this exercise often.**

→ Pick a goal from one area of your life. Picture it in detail.

→ Imagine stepping into the "you" in the picture and actually experiencing your achievement of that goal. Notice how it feels, what you see, hear, and think. Notice how other people treat you.

→ Look into the future beyond your achievement of the goal. How does achieving this goal benefit all areas of your life?

→ Look back at the past and your route to achieving your goal. Note your successes and the obstacles you overcame. Notice how different they are now that you have overcome them. Appreciate how you feel about your achievements.

→ Imagine yourself walking backwards from your future achievement to the present. Notice what resources you needed and what you learned from specific steps you took to help you along the way.

→ From the present look forwards to your goal and appreciate the journey. Map out key stages of the journey and the resources you require right now.

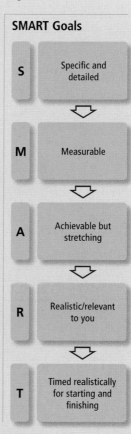

**SMART Goals**

| | |
|---|---|
| **S** | Specific and detailed |
| **M** | Measurable |
| **A** | Achievable but stretching |
| **R** | Realistic/relevant to you |
| **T** | Timed realistically for starting and finishing |

# Summary: Get on the Right Path

If you are to achieve success with your projects you will need to motivate the members of your team. Learn how to motivate others by tapping in to the great motivational theories. Create and sustain motivation by utilizing new strategies and information. Be clear about what you expect of people and encourage them to break their bad habits.

## Utilizing Your Resources

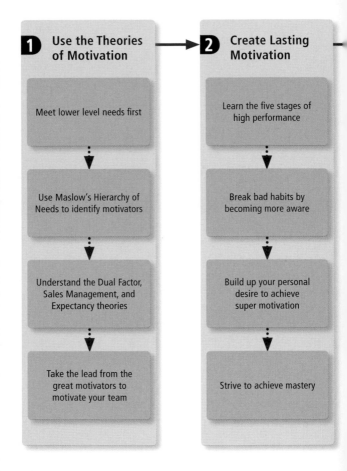

**1 Use the Theories of Motivation**

Meet lower level needs first

Use Maslow's Hierarchy of Needs to identify motivators

Understand the Dual Factor, Sales Management, and Expectancy theories

Take the lead from the great motivators to motivate your team

**2 Create Lasting Motivation**

Learn the five stages of high performance

Break bad habits by becoming more aware

Build up your personal desire to achieve super motivation

Strive to achieve mastery

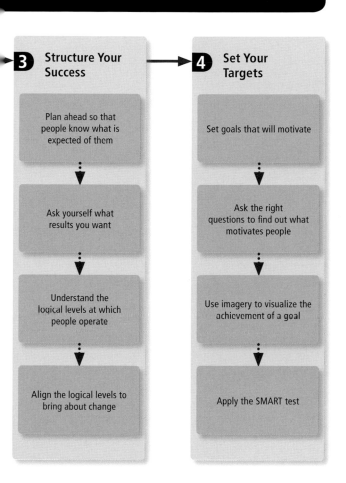

**3** **Structure Your Success**

Plan ahead so that people know what is expected of them

Ask yourself what results you want

Understand the logical levels at which people operate

Align the logical levels to bring about change

**4** **Set Your Targets**

Set goals that will motivate

Ask the right questions to find out what motivates people

Use imagery to visualize the achievement of a goal

Apply the SMART test

# Manage with Motivation

In today's competitive marketplace finding and locating motivated staff is difficult. Once you have found them, managing them and sustaining their motivation is equally challenging. This chapter focuses on how to attract, manage, and retain the most motivated people. It will demonstrate:

- Why it's important that you attract the best
- How to organize training and development that rewards and inspires
- Why motivational meetings are essential for building a high performance team
- How to create lasting motivation.

# Get the Right People on Board

Successful recruitment requires careful planning and consideration. By recruiting and selecting the right people to work in your organization you will be able to develop a highly motivated team.

## Identify the Role

It is essential to specify the role for which you are recruiting. If you are to attract the right people you will need to put a lot of thought into the job description, the purpose of the role, and the kind of person who will best perform this role in the context of your organization.
A written job description is useful, not only for external agencies working with you, but also as a way of keeping aligned the different people involved internally in the organization's recruitment process. A personal specification may also be useful – this is something that can easily be incorporated into the job description.

## think SMART

**!**

**Good management is not simply about motivating existing team members; it's your ability to motivate potential team members that will determine whether you get the right people on board in the first place.**

If you can't offer potential employees or team members a reason to join your organization, you won't attract the quality of candidates that you need to develop a highly motivated team. Before recruiting new staff, think about what your organization can offer them, plan properly for interviews and provide feedback.

"**If the ladder is not leaning against the right wall, every step we take just takes us to the wrong place faster.**
Steven Covey"

## Attract Talent

The key to creating a motivated team is to attract the right people to your organization. The more attractive you are to potential staff, the more choice you will have when recruiting.

→ Internal recruitment is a valuable source of talent, is cost effective, and provides an opportunity to promote, reward, and recognize effort and performance. Advertise on notice boards, intranet, staff newsletters, and at internal meetings.

→ Referrals offer a cost-effective and highly targeted way of reaching competent staff. You could create a referral scheme that would reward your existing staff for the successful recruitment of new team members.

→ Place your own advertisements and run your own campaigns. Consider newspapers, trade periodicals, graduate schemes, job centres, and open days.

→ Use professional recruitment organizations – whether on an ad hoc basis or in partnership. The services offered and received from external agencies vary dramatically and you should do some research prior to making a decision.

### Know Who You Want

The objective of a personal specification is to consider the personal attributes, experience, and capabilities of the right person. Personal specifications will often be split into mandatory and desirable criteria.

- **Physical requirements** – Speech, general appearance, manner, fitness
- **Achievements** – Education, qualifications, experience, past successes
- **Personal qualities relevant to the job –** Empathy, communication skills, motivation
- **Personality** – Ability to fit in to the existing team
- **Interests** – Activities relevant to the ability to do the job

## Know Your Options

The quality of your selection process will determine not only whether you choose the right staff but also whether they decide to work for your organization. Having a pre-defined, objective process creates a professional and efficient way of ensuring that you get the right people into your organization. There are several selection tools, all of which are effective in different situations when utilized by experienced individuals who have been properly trained.

- **Selection interviews** can be carried out with one or more interviewers. They are the most widely utilized selection tool when recruiting.
- **Assessment centres** are becoming increasingly popular, particularly for managerial, professional, and graduate positions. They can provide several candidates at once and have been shown to be an effective predictor of a candidate's future success. Assessment centres will generally carry out written tests, one-to-one interviews, group exercises and activities, and presentations.

**Practise Your Technique**
If you've never conducted an interview before, practise on a friend or colleague, taking note of weak areas as you proceed.

## Plan the Perfect Interview

**HIGH IMPACT**

- Writing a clear job description
- Reading the candidate's CV in advance of the interview and researching former employers
- Greeting interviewees and starting the interview punctually
- Preparing your interview
- Giving timely feedback and following up after the interview
- Ensuring that all procedures are fair and legal

**NEGATIVE IMPACT**

- Failing to plan properly
- Reading the candidate's CV for the first time while you are conducting the interview
- Leaving interviewees waiting; failing to reserve an appropriate interview location
- Running an unplanned interview
- Failing to give feedback
- Showing bias or ignoring legal requirements

---

- **Psychological testing** is focused either on attainment/ ability/general intelligence and psychometric questionnaires or on personality tests. This latter group includes tests such as Myers-Brigs and the Holdsworth Occupational Personality Questionnaire. To run and utilize the output data from psychological testing requires professional training.

> **A good selection process will produce the right result**

- **Panel interviews** are often utilized when recruiting people for high-pressure jobs or competitive situations. Despite their somewhat archaic qualities they can be an effective way of putting candidates under pressure. The way in which someone responds to this pressure will demonstrate to the interviewers whether he has the qualities required for the role for which he is being recruited.
- **Role-playing** can be used to simulate the work environment and to gain an insight into the candidate's behaviours and habits at work.

# Training and Development

Structured training and development programmes are essential for the development of long-term morale and motivation. Whenever people are asked what motivates them personal development features highly.

## Make Training Ongoing

Whether you need to train staff on a new piece of equipment, increase existing skills, or improve weak skills, training is vital to the success of the modern organization. If you want people to see development programmes as being worthwhile they need to be ongoing and consistent. Key to the success of any development programme is the training needs analysis. Completed prior to training, this does not have to be expensive or time consuming. It's important to think of managerial training, too. Many organizations invest heavily in staff development but fail to develop their managers adequately.

## Find the Right Trainer

The expertise of the trainer or coach, internal or external, appointed to develop and run training courses is of paramount importance. If you get this right, you're far more likely to be running a successful course that will have long-term benefits, both for the participants and for the organization.

### Tailor Your Approach

Starting with an individual department or team ask yourself what the primary business objectives of that team are

Make a list of the core behaviours that you want the team to demonstrate and the core skills that are required to do this

Now rate the team on how effectively it executes the core behaviours currently

Once you have identified the "gaps", decide whether the gap in behaviour is driven by lack of skills, lack of motivation, or both

# Find the Right Format

Once the decision has been taken regarding the subject matter for the development programme it is important that the programme is delivered in the most efficient format possible.

| Developmental Format | Pros | Cons |
|---|---|---|
| **Group training** | Builds team spirit, is cost effective, and uses a standard approach | Individuals have different learning styles and needs, training requires time out of the office |
| **One-to-one coaching** | Personalized and tailored, timely, and adjusts delivery/speed | Takes time and can sometimes lack energy |
| **On the job training** | Time-effective, focused and relevant, easy to do "in-house" | Can build on bad habits and is easily forgotten or postponed |
| **Mentoring** | Grows internal talent, uses existing experience/skills within the organization, and is contextually accurate | Can build on established bad habits, may miss external solutions, and can stifle individual responsibility |
| **E-learning** | Cheap, easy, and quick, can be studied in your own time, and requires no trainer/coach | May not get done properly, will not suit some, and misses out on important personal elements |
| **Self-learning – books, audios, DVDs** | Cheap and easy, can be studied in your own time, and may not require a coach or trainer | Will not suit some, requires self-discipline, and will need contextualizing for your organization |
| **External seminars and workshops** | You'll meet other people, it's delivered by experts, and is cost effective for smaller numbers | Requires time out of office, and is difficult to follow through without knowledge of the content |
| **Teleseminars** | Cheap and easy, quick and effective, and can be delivered internally or externally | No face-to-face contact and may not be taken seriously by some |

# Design Your Training Session

This is your presentation arena, so control it! Prepare for the unexpected wherever you are. Creating your own checklist will reduce the likelihood of having to deal with eventualities for which you are unprepared.

→ Remember to take into the account the different types of people who will attend your presentation and devise methods that will engage them fully.

→ You will have to appeal to visual, auditory and kinaesthetic people, so tailor your language to all three types.

→ If you see that people's attention is wandering during your presentation, be prepared to change the focus to get them interested in what you are saying.

## Factor in the Variables

| Factor | Suggestions |
|---|---|
| **Visual people** | Use flip charts, videos, models, PowerPoints, and handouts to engage people who will like to "see" the point you are making. |
| **Auditory people** | Make sure that you speak clearly and that you express your emotions when talking. Facilitate group discussions. |
| **Kinaesthetic people** | Create models that they can use. Run practical exercises. Give handouts that they can touch. |
| **Why?** | Explain why this training is important and link it to both performance and reward. |
| **What?** | Provide statistics, facts, and case studies. Make sure that you back up your case with solid facts. |
| **How?** | Let individuals have a go. Involve them in exercises and role-plays. Encourage participation. |
| **What if?** | Encourage brainstorming, action planning and planning for the future. |
| **Breaks** | Allow adequate breaks for those who have short attention spans and require regular breaks. |

## Prepare Thoroughly

Learning to deliver a powerful training session will have a significant effect on increasing the levels of motivation in your organization by improving the overall effectiveness of any programme that is run. Take into account the audience and any training needs analysis that has taken place. Training in the right subjects at the right level is essential if you are to keep delegates engaged. Asking "What subjects would be useful for these delegates?" and "What is the best format for this training?" will set you on the right track. The structure of the training should be outlined, with core subjects broken down.

## Control the Session

Speak clearly and confidently and use the whole range of your voice. Maintain good eye contact. If you haven't done much presenting it's a good idea to practise. This will help you to feel more confident and allow you to get your timings right. Take questions at the end of your presentation. Stay calm and take all questions confidently. Even challenging questions show that your audience is still interested! If you don't know the answer, "buy" time by throwing the answer out to another member of the audience or by seeking further clarification from the questioner. Try saying something like, "That's an interesting question, John, let's find out what the others think. Mary, what's your take on that?" Whatever you do, don't try to bluff if you don't have the facts.

## 5 minute FIX

If you are called on to run a training session at short notice and with little preparation, jot down five points against each of the following questions:

- What would you like the delegates to do differently as a result of the session?

- What will help support them in their new behaviours?

- How will you engage with them?

- How will you go about encouraging their interaction?

## Plan for Success

It is important that you know how you are going to follow up on training sessions to create sustainability and ongoing benefits for your organization. People need to know how training will benefit them and how it will affect their overall performance and the results that they are getting. They also need to know how they will be rewarded for improvement. Pre-course objectives need to be set for all training programmes. People who know why they are attending training and what they need to get out of it are more focused and motivated during the training.

## Follow Through

People also need to know how you plan to debrief them after training, what they will be expected to do differently as a result of the training, and how you will support them afterwards. A meeting should be held after the programme so that they can discuss with you how well they have met their objectives and what they now need to do to put their learning into practise. You will need to arrange a suitable time to review this progress and to decide upon the next steps to be taken.

**Learn to Work Together**
When team members are having difficulty working as a group, a training session can help them to discover how they can work together to achieve success.

# Case study: Changing Training Outcomes

A media sales agency ran training courses to motivate team members and increase skills levels. No pre-course conversations took place and people often attended training without having been given any objectives. Not knowing why they were present or how the course would benefit them, they felt that they could be doing other things that would be a better use of their time. Management saw training courses as expensive and ineffective. The management team decided to sit down with the team members individually prior to training to discuss what they wanted to get out of the training and how they would implement what they learned, and again after training to support them in implementing their action plans.

• *When the management team realized that they needed to support training they were able to put the right structures in place.*
• *People attending the training courses began to take responsibility for their own development and better results were soon being achieved.*

## Pass It On

One of the best ways of helping people to retain information is to make them aware that they will be required to teach it to others later. Decide with the attendees prior to a training course that they will be running a short course for their colleagues afterwards to pass on the information and training that they have received. You could use these training mini-sessions run by individual team members to add variety to morning meetings and regular training sessions. Encouraging the members of your team to take responsibility for their own development in this way will help them to build a good team spirit, so that they will learn to work together well, increasing their effectiveness and productivity.

**Effective training will improve motivation**

# Run Motivational Meetings

Learning to plan, design, and run regular meetings is an important part of team and individual motivation. Good meetings can be a powerful source of inspiration and will promote good team bonding.

## Participate Fully

An effective meeting is one that is planned and has a definite purpose. It is highly participative and encourages individuals to get involved and to voice their opinions. It is viewed as an opportunity to discuss problems and challenges, analyze situations, brainstorm solutions, and discuss best practice. It is also a meeting that is regular, timely, and consistent in content and quality.

## Avoid Disturbances

Keep the door of the meeting room closed and attach a notice to the effect that a meeting is in progress. Make sure that the office and the phones are covered and that people not involved in the meeting understand that they cannot disturb you unless it is critical. This will help to ensure that people who need to be present won't have a reason to excuse themselves during the meeting.

## think
### SMART

**You need to ensure that you are fully prepared for your meeting. If you do not approach this seriously, neither will the members of your team.**

Your preparation does not need to take long but it is essential. In addition to the content of your meeting, ensure that you have considered room layout, handouts/brochures/paperwork, notepads and pens, PowerPoint presentation materials, electricity points, lighting, heating, housekeeping issues (fire exits, toilets, etc.), flip charts, pens, breaks, refreshments.

# Plan Your Motivational Meeting

**Despite the fact that most managers spend an increasing amount of time in meetings, many do not run regular meetings for their staff.**

The main reasons for this are lack of planning, lack of experience, lack of belief, and bad experiences in the past. Ask yourself:

→ What is the purpose of having a regular meeting?
→ When is the best time to hold your meeting? How regularly are you going to run your meetings?
→ What do you want your team to get out of the meetings? What do you think is the best way to facilitate this outcome?
→ How can you get your team involved in the meetings?
→ What is the best way for your team to share positive experiences and best practice?
→ Where is the best location for your meetings? How long do you think your meetings should last?
→ What resources/props do you need for your meetings?
→ How can you ensure that your meetings will stay fresh and motivational in the long term? What action can you take if people start to lose interest in the proceedings?

| |
|---|
| PLAN |

⬇

| |
|---|
| PREPARE |

⬇

| |
|---|
| FACILITATE |

⬇

| |
|---|
| SHARE |

**Make the Most of Meetings** Plan and run meetings properly, encouraging sharing, to maximize the benefits.

**TIP** Motivate yourself before you start the meeting. You cannot produce positive emotions in your staff simply by going through the motions.

## Be Positive

Every meeting should be a positive anchor for the kinds of attitudes and behaviours that you want to see in the organization on a day-to-day basis. One of the main reasons that managers decide to stop running regular meetings or do not place enough importance on their meetings is that they are not getting the results that they want. Every meeting should be a positive and dynamic experience. There are several meeting strategies and techniques that you can tailor to help you to get the most out of your regular meetings.

- **Agenda** – Set a brief agenda for the meeting so that people know what is going to be covered and how long the meeting will last.
- **Follow-ups** – It is important that you follow through; and each meeting should include a progress report on actions from the last meeting.
- **Mini-training sessions** – These can be run by you or by one of your team. They are usually five to 15 minutes in length and are designed to deliver new information, review old information, and/or expand on existing skills. Keep this session participative and include follow-up checks and activities.

**Change the Format** If your team members are showing signs of boredom during meetings, do something unusual to liven them up.

## Dynamic Meeting Strategies

**HIGH IMPACT**

- Knowing your objectives
- Planning the structure of your meetings
- Involving the whole team
- Scheduling meetings
- Taking action and following through after meetings

**NEGATIVE IMPACT**

- Having no real purpose for your meeting
- Ad libbing throughout meetings
- Failing to invite all team members to meetings
- Cancelling/postponing meetings
- Chatting aimlessly

---

- **High-energy activities** – Lasting for anything from 30 seconds to five minutes, these activities are designed to produce energy and promote fun and activity by creating movement – try a role-play, a simple stretching exercise, or even a Mexican wave! People will feel re-energized and refreshed afterwards.
- **Problem solving** – Ask everyone to write on a sheet of paper one problem that they would like solutions/suggestions for. Pass the sheets of paper around the meeting and ask everyone to write down on each one a suggestion for dealing with the problem. Pass each sheet back to the original owner for action. As an alternative you could split those attending the meeting into two teams and have each team present the other with a problem that it would like to have solved. Each team would then have ten minutes to come up with solutions that it would present to the other team.
- **Brainstorming** – This is an opportunity for people to focus on an outcome that they want and to share ideas on how to achieve it. The ideas produced can be actioned immediately or may lead to further research and actions on a particular issue.

---

**The only limit to your impact is your imagination and commitment.** Anthony Robbins

# Reward Excellence

**Reward is an essential tool for keeping people properly motivated. People expect rewards to be fair and related to the effort that they have put in.**

## Consider the Variables

Rewards management is a complex subject that focuses on creating, maintaining, and communicating a reward system that motivates people to achieve high performance. Different approaches and variables need to be taken into account in order to put into place a well-thought-out reward scheme for your team.

## Key Questions to Ask About Rewards

What you perceive to be a fair rewards package will depend very much on your own perceptions. When designing rewards it is important that you are aware of your own beliefs about rewards.

- Should people be rewarded for the jobs that they do or for the skills and capabilities that they have?
- Should rewards be based upon people's seniority or their performance?
- Should your organization's perceived position in the market place make any difference to the rewards given?

# Case study: Getting People Involved

Rory, a senior manager, took on his new role to turn around an under-performing team. In his initial meetings he discovered that the team members were unhappy with elements of their rewards packages. They felt that these were unfair and not competitive within the industry. With the contribution of the team Rory revised the packages and increased motivation and results within the organization.

- *Getting the staff involved in the rewards process made them feel appreciated and involved.*
- *Changing the basis on which rewards packages were put together was good for the team and for the organization.*

## Types of Reward

There are many different types of reward, and it is essential to understand what someone's motivators are before you decide which reward is appropriate for that person:

→ **Money** – Commission, pay increase, bonus, profit-related pay, car allowance, fuel allowance
→ **Training/development** – Personal or professional training
→ **Equipment/kit** – Laptop computers, mobile phones, electronic organizers, company cars, uniforms
→ **Loans** – Loans for season tickets for travel or other allowances
→ **Tangible gifts** – Vouchers, cinema or theatre tickets, bottle of wine, portable music player
→ **Away days** – Team or organization events such as go-karting, a meal out, bowling, paint-balling
→ **Non-salary financial benefits** – Health insurance, pension contributions, share schemes, dental insurance, paid petrol
→ **Personal benefits** – Free crèche, increased holiday entitlement, events with partner/family, gym membership
→ **Recognition** – Hand-written note, mention in company newsletter, a simple "thank you"

- Should other organizations and industries be checked to ensure that similar rewards are in place?
- Should rewards be determined centrally (e.g. by group HR), or locally by managers?
- Should your position in the hierarchy of your business determine your salary?
- Should one person's reward be related to the success of another on the team?

Although there are no "right" answers to any of these questions, they are important issues for you to address when designing a rewards package for your organization. The most important factor to take into account is the motivators of the people who will be rewarded.

## Encourage Results

When designing rewards schemes it is important that you consider the individuals on your teams and the culture of your business in order to get the best results. Studies have shown that employees value rewards schemes and packages that reflect their efforts and their results. Fixed and rewards-based packages are universally recognized as important for salespeople but can be equally important for others too. It is important to understand that the deciding factor in whether a reward is high value or low value is the perception of the recipients themselves. What is considered high value in one business or for one team may be considered low value for another team or within a different business, and the most effective reward in a particular industry may be very inexpensive to provide.

**Do Your Research** If you are going to motivate effectively you will need to be aware of the reward culture that operates in your organization.

---

**Rewards Checklist**

We have both a fixed and a variable reward scheme ☐

We have considered the rewards variables and decided what is important to our organization ☐

We have rewards schemes for sales and non-sales people ☐

Our rewards benefit those who act in alignment with the behaviours that we expect from our staff ☐

We have included low cost/high value and high cost/high value rewards and have reduced low cost/low value and high cost/low value rewards ☐

Our rewards are fair and equitable and reward both performance and results ☐

## Understand the Four Types of Reward

**The cost of a reward is fixed, but whether a reward is high or low value will always be determined by the person to whom the reward is being given.**

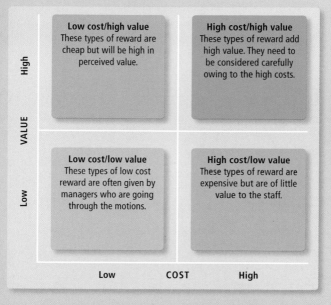

→ **Low cost/high value** – Cinema or theatre tickets or a bottle of wine as a daily prize can be very motivational.

→ **High cost/high value** – These can and should form a significant part of a good rewards package. They would include pension schemes or health insurance.

→ **High cost/low value** – This might be a share scheme that allows staff to own part of the organization but which is perceived as a right rather than a bonus. This would be expensive, but would not be motivational.

→ **Low cost/low value** – Vouchers or breakfast in the office. Positioned wrongly they will have no motivational value, and may even demotivate.

# Summary: Developing Your Team

Recruiting the right people is key to creating a motivated team. Establish good recruitment procedures and learn effective interview techniques. Set up training procedures and run motivational meetings that will inspire your team. Finally, understand the reward culture in your organization and reward team members appropriately.

## Running a Tight Ship

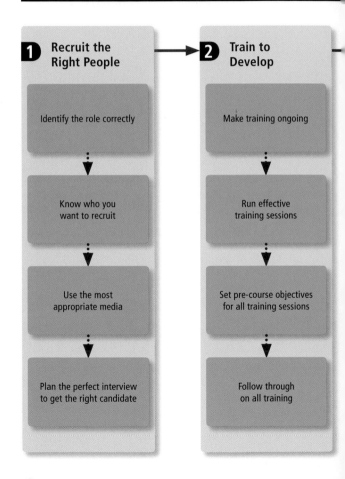

**1 Recruit the Right People**

Identify the role correctly

Know who you want to recruit

Use the most appropriate media

Plan the perfect interview to get the right candidate

**2 Train to Develop**

Make training ongoing

Run effective training sessions

Set pre-course objectives for all training sessions

Follow through on all training

**3** Run Meetings that Motivate

Plan and design regular meetings

⋮

Make your meetings dynamic

⋮

Prepare thoroughly and encourage full participation

⋮

Follow through from one meeting to the next

**4** Use Reward as a Motivator

Make sure you reward excellence

⋮

Become aware of the organization's reward culture

⋮

Reward consistently and in line with what motivates people

⋮

Determine the value of a reward to different people

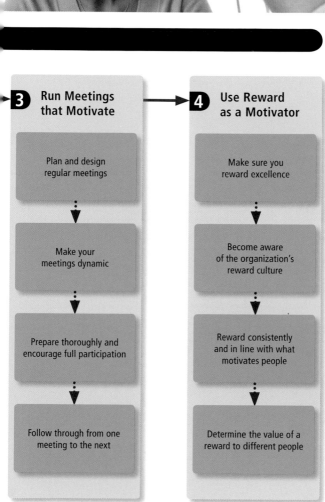

# Listen to 4
## Learn

Many people think that motivation is
something that you give to people, but in
fact it comes from within. As a motivator
your role is to understand the members of
your team and to help them to motivate
themselves. This chapter looks at some of
the core strategies for fully understanding
people and helping them to get the results
that they want. You will learn:

- How to run simple but effective coaching
  sessions that will build lasting motivation
- The art of asking questions that focus
  people on results
- How to listen effectively
- How to position feedback as "the food
  of champions".

# Be a Good Coach

**A coach helps people to improve their performance and motivation by empowering them to set and achieve goals and create sustainable increases in performance.**

## Understand What Coaching Is

Coaching has elements of several different disciplines and can often be confused with them.

- **Mentoring** is the teaching of skills for a specific role. Mentors will usually have worked in the role for which they are mentoring someone and will understand the "ins and outs" of that role.
- **Consulting** is seeking the advice of experts on specific issues. Coaches are expected to draw on their own resources to formulate their own answers.
- **Counselling** is guidance in dealing with personal or social problems. Counselling is more about dealing with problems whereas coaching is about finding solutions.
- **Therapy** focuses on dealing with psychological issues. If therapy is required then the coach should refer the coachee to a fully qualified practitioner.

## Assess Your Coaching Skills

Use this test as a benchmark to see where you can grow and develop and become a better coach and motivator.

Read these statements and rate yourself from 1 to 5, where **1** = untrue **2** = usually untrue **3** = neutral **4** = usually true **5** = absolutely true.

| | |
|---|---|
| I am interested in individuals and ask questions to understand more about people. | I invest in my own personal development – books, audio-visual aids, and training. |
| I listen to individuals carefully, trying to understand what they mean. | I am prepared to challenge others when appropriate. |
| I am focused on outcomes and oriented towards solutions. | I view mistakes as something to learn from. |
| I am a positive individual and know how to motivate myself. | I am tuned in to what people are really thinking. |

## Coaches are Motivators

Good motivators are also excellent coaches who can develop people's abilities. Simply listening and encouraging people to present their ideas, for example, can really help them to learn.

**Increase Motivation**
Coaches increase motivation by asking the right questions and listening to what people have to say, encouraging them to embrace change and learn from any mistakes they make.

**Empower People**
Creating a supportive coaching environment will empower individuals so that they are open and receptive to developmental feedback and keen to take action to improve their skills.

**Encourage Learning**
Good coaches use all of the resources within their team to help individuals develop – in this case, using third party feedback from another team member to get a different perspective.

# GROW Your Talent

The GROW model is a powerful tool for helping people to move from being problem focused to being solution oriented. GROW is one of the most widely used coaching models because it produces good results.

## Who Are You?

The GROW model is only as effective as the coach using it. While it is worth considering which coaching style, model, or approach might be best for you and your teams it is worth noting that many of the best coaches are the best because of "who" they are as opposed to what they studied. You could think of applying the techniques used by a mentor you admire to improve your results. Although the GROW model may appear to be a sequential model it is, in fact, far less linear than it looks. Coach and coachee may start anywhere within the model and could cover each stage several times. Revisiting the model during the session will help the coach to identify where she should be focusing her attention to get the best result.

## think SMART

!

**An effective coaching technique is to ask your question and then remain silent until you receive an answer. The longer it takes the coachee to answer, the more powerful the answer will usually be.**

Inexperienced managers often answer coachees' questions for them. Allow the coachee to arrive at her own conclusion, even if it is not the one that you had anticipated. Avoid making assumptions and asking questions in such a way that the answer is a foregone conclusion. Utilize the GROW model to fully explore every option. Check that your coachee has been completely honest about her current reality – if she hasn't, it will be difficult for her to grow and develop.

## Use the GROW Model

**There is a proliferation of coaching techniques and strategies and these styles and approaches have their own strengths and weaknesses. Using the simple GROW model well can be a powerful tool for change.**

### → Goals

What is it that you specifically want to achieve?

How will you know when you have achieved this?

Why is achieving it important to you?

Do you believe this is achievable?

How committed are you to this goal?

### → Reality

What is your current situation?

What is holding you back at the moment?

What actions have you taken so far?

How successful have they been?

What did you learn from them?

### → Options

What options are available to you?

What would a peak performer do in this situation?

What would you do if failure simply wasn't an option?

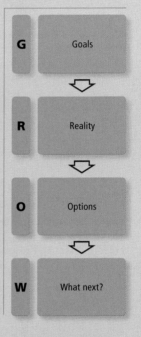

How have you encountered and solved similar challenges before?

What would you do if you had all of the resources (such as time, money, expertise) in the world?

### → What Next?

What actions are you going to take?

When are you going to start/stop? How long will it take?

What challenges might you face?

How are you going to deal with them?

What resources do you need to achieve your goal?

# Motivate with Questions

**The questions you ask focus your thoughts and determine whether you are motivated or not. By studying motivational questioning techniques you can dramatically improve your motivational skills.**

## Ask Good Questions

Many people think that the art of a great motivator is delivering powerful and inspiring rhetoric but the power of questions outweighs this. In today's blame culture many of the questions that are asked are framed negatively:

- Whose fault was that?
- Who can we blame?
- What went wrong?

While these problem-focused questions may be important for an analysis of performance they are not an effective way of motivating people.

**Good questions produce better answers**

## Practise on Yourself

Your questions should always be focused on the solution or outcome that you want. You should always think carefully before you ask a question. Three of the most powerful questions that you can ask are:

- What do you want to achieve?
- What can you learn from this?
- How can you constantly improve what you do?

The more focused your questions are, the more specific will be the responses you receive to them. The answers to these questions should enable you to assess what your own priorities are and point you towards a course of action that will allow you to achieve a better quality of life.

> **Successful people ask better questions, and as a result, they get better answers.**
>
> Anthony Robbins

## Using the GROW Model

Open questions are those that cannot easily be answered with a simple "yes" or "no". Most people ask more closed questions than open questions, so it is crucial that you plan properly and prepare your questions properly before you begin working with someone. Consider the quality of information each of the questions below will elicit:

- Did your motivation problem start when you were late for work last week?
- Do you think your target is achievable?
- How could you take more responsibility for your personal motivation on a day-to-day basis?
- Have you written your forecasts for next month yet?
- What strategies could be implemented in order to improve customer service levels?
- What would you like to have achieved by this time next year?
- Are you going to take charge of this project?
- What actions do you think you could take to improve your performance right now?

## Ask the Right Questions

The first word of a sentence will usually indicate whether the question is going to be open or closed. Sentences starting with words such as could, should, did, would, have, had, are, is, will, couldn't, shouldn't, wouldn't, etc. are closed questions and require only "yes" or "no" answers. Open questions start with how, where, when, what, which, why, who, what if.

### The Value of the Right Type of Question

| CLOSED QUESTIONS | OPEN QUESTIONS |
|---|---|
| • Require only "yes" or "no" answers | • Require detailed answers |
| • Limit information gathering | • Produce more information of a better quality |
| • Fail to explore possibilities | • Unlock possibilities |

## Ask the Right Questions

The subject matter of your questions is as important as the structure of the questions. Great motivators know what to ask questions about and what not to ask questions about in order to get the information they want.

## Make Challenging Statements

In order to challenge limiting statements you need to encourage the person making the statement to see the situation from a different perspective.

| Statement | Challenge |
|-----------|-----------|
| You can't be motivated all of the time. | Who says you can't? What would happen if you were? |
| This environment demotivates me. | How exactly does the environment cause you to choose to feel demotivated? |
| She's always moaning. She thinks I'm worthless. | How does her moaning mean that she thinks that you're worthless? Have you ever moaned at someone you thought was worthwhile? |
| If my boss knew how hard I worked she would appreciate me more. | How do you know she doesn't know? How do you know she doesn't appreciate you? |
| They always complain about our work. | Has there ever been a time when they didn't complain? |
| I can't do that. | What would happen if you did? How could you do that? |
| Motivation around here is non-existent. | What would you need to do to increase motivation levels? |
| She doesn't rate me. | How do you know? What would you do if you pretended she did? |
| There's nothing I can do about it. | Nothing? If there were one thing, what would it be? |
| It's always the same; you can't change it. | How do you know you can't change it? What if you could change it? Has there ever been a time when it was different? |

## Ask Three Important Questions

One of the most important factors when someone is seeking personal change is her perception of change

**Be Positive** Motivate someone by encouraging her to acknowledge the importance of what it is she hopes to achieve.

and the value that she places on the change. Ask her:
- How important is it for you to make this change on a scale of 1–10?
- How important is this change to you?
- How confident are you that when you set your mind to it you will be able to achieve your goals?

## Challenge Limitations

When spending any amount of time working one-on-one with someone it is important that your conversation has structure and purpose. Listen carefully for potential motivational blocks and challenge them through intelligent questioning. A statement such as, "No one can be motivated all of the time" needs to be challenged as it will become a potentially limiting factor.

---

**TIP** Write down five limiting statements that you have heard from members of your team. Create five challenges to deconstruct the blocks to motivation.

---

# Listen to Understand

Think about a time when someone listened to you without any agenda. Did this motivate you? If you're going to learn to listen properly you need to know what being listened to properly feels like.

## Learn to Listen

When combined with good questioning techniques, listening is sometimes all that is required to motivate someone to solve her own problems. One of the key skills of being a good motivator is that of being a good listener. Few of us have ever been taught to listen properly. We rarely focus on our listening techniques but are offended if someone tells us that we are bad listeners.

## 5 minute FIX

**Many managers listen in order to talk. Plan to listen to understand:**

- Write down some questions before you start working with someone.

- Write down some answers and practise asking yourself questions about them.

- Practise avoiding phrases such as, "What I think is…", and "The way I see it".

## Listen Effectively

**HIGH IMPACT**

- Building rapport and understanding
- Unlocking personal drivers
- Understanding beliefs and values
- Encouraging free expression
- Engendering good team spirit and co-operation
- Motivating individuals and teams
- Developing emotional awareness
- Encouraging personal responsibility

**NEGATIVE IMPACT**

- "Turning off" from the speaker
- Ignoring the individual
- Making assumptions
- Silencing opinion
- Creating resistance and hostility in people
- Allowing negativity to demotivate people
- Stunting personal development
- Creating dependence and fostering lack of responsibility

## The Nine Levels of Listening

If you don't listen properly your attempts at motivation will be based on trial and error, conjecture, and guesswork. In order to discover exactly how people are motivated you need to ask questions and then listen. There are nine listening levels, ranging from inattentiveness to full attention on the listener's part. If you're operating at a low level, try to improve the quality of your listening, so that you will be better able to motivate people.

## Improve Your Concentration

Improving your listening skills is not easy. We usually listen out of our conscious awareness most of the time, so improving results means breaking existing habits. The benefits, however, are exceptional, not only when motivating others but also in other areas of life. You will be able to achieve so much more when people say to you, "You know, I really think that you understand me!"

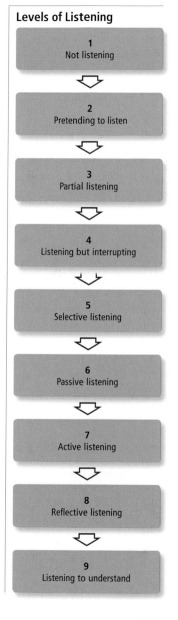

### Levels of Listening

1 Not listening

2 Pretending to listen

3 Partial listening

4 Listening but interrupting

5 Selective listening

6 Passive listening

7 Active listening

8 Reflective listening

9 Listening to understand

# Be Present When Listening

When you start to listen properly you will realize that you are beginning to get a far deeper understanding of the people you are trying to motivate as they will be more open and honest with you.

## See Things from Another Perspective

When you communicate you interpret what others are saying through your own filtering system so that it makes sense to you. Many managers rush in to "fix" motivational problems without ever really understanding the underlying factors as the other person sees them. How many times have you been having a conversation and, before the other person has finished, you think, "I know what she means here, I can sort this out"? In order to listen well you need to train yourself to silence your own inner dialogue so that you can concentrate fully on what the other person is saying and understand how they really feel.

**Learn to Listen** Take time out to silence what is going on inside your head, so that you will be able to listen to someone else with your full attention.

## TECHNIQUES *to* practise

**Reflective listening is a guess about the meaning of what someone is saying.** It requires a constant focus on the meaning behind the words. "I wish I were more motivated" could mean "I'm depressed and unhappy with my job" or "I find your style of management frustrating"! Next time you're having a discussion, try using this technique.

- Reflect the speaker's words by repeating them back – "You wish you were more motivated." It is important to deliver the reflection using a downward or level inflection at the end of the sentence rather than an upward one, which would turn your statement into a question.
- Rephrase the wording of whatever the speaker has just said – "You can't find time to work on the project that we discussed."
- Add some emotion to what you are saying – "You're feeling down because you can't find time to work on the project we discussed."

## Be Honest

Be honest with yourself about your listening skills. How well do you listen? How well do you focus on others when they are talking? Just because you know how to listen doesn't mean that you do it properly. While your listening skills will not change from moment to moment, your use of them will. You will probably demonstrate different levels of listening at different times and in different circumstances. This may fluctuate according to your mood, the environment, your stress levels, your priorities, and how interested you are in the other person. Before you meet someone, visualize yourself really listening to understand.

> **Every person I work with knows something better than me. My job is to listen long enough to find it and use it.**
>
> Jack Nichols

# Give Good Feedback

**Giving consistent feedback is highly motivational and is crucial for business success. Learning to give the right sort of feedback to people will greatly improve your ability to motivate others effectively.**

## Believe in Feedback

Peak performers see feedback as "the food of champions" and they use this information to measure their progress and adjust behaviours. Without feedback, any personal assessment of progress can be difficult. Managers give many reasons for not giving feedback:

- People see criticism, even when constructive, as failure
- It feels just telling people off
- People don't like negative feedback
- Feedback can be taken the wrong way
- It's difficult to give positively
- I don't have enough time
- They already know how they are doing.

If feedback is given in the wrong way, these objections may sometimes arise. The key is to make sure that your feedback always follows the right formula.

## Effective Ways to Criticise Constructively

**HIGH IMPACT**

- Last week you were late twice. This disappoints me.
- You have missed your targets for this quarter by 25 per cent. This makes me rather worried about your real commitment to this organization.
- You failed to log off the system twice last week. I wonder if you understand the importance of logging on and off?

**NEGATIVE IMPACT**

- You're never on time. I think that you are getting lazy.
- You never deliver on schedule. I don't think you're good enough to do this job.
- You're lazy and incompetent, you never listen, and you never do what you're asked to do.
- You always go your own way. Why can't you understand that it ruins things for others?

## Rules for Giving Feedback

Feedback must be based on observed facts about behaviour in order to prevent people taking the message personally and becoming resistant. It must never be about them as people. Once the feedback has been given you should listen to what the person has to say before asking her what she thinks a more appropriate action might be, or suggesting one yourself.

→ Always have a positive intention.
→ Give feedback on behaviours, not people.
→ Give feedback at the time.
→ Use specific examples.
→ Only use first person examples, not third person examples and second-hand opinions.
→ Be consistent and accurate.

### Create a Learning Environment

Encourage the giving and receiving of feedback where learning is paramount and failure is seen in a positive light. Key to this approach is that the intention behind the feedback is positive. Feedback is designed to let people know how they are doing, help them to improve their performance, open a coaching dialogue, and allow them to express any concerns and worries.

### The Core Components of Effective Feedback

When giving effective feedback there are three core components: the intention behind the feedback, your positive control of your current emotional state, and the content and structure of your message. Feedback given in anger or retaliation will never be received positively. Even if the message you are conveying in your feedback is difficult for the recipient of the feedback to hear, make it calmly and reasonably and be prepared to listen to the response.

# Praise Your Team

**Praising people is essential to fostering long-term motivation. People consistently rate being given praise as one of the key motivational factors in the workplace.**

## Give Feedback Immediately

Praise seems to be something that many managers are unwilling or unable to give. They are often very quick to criticize and reluctant to give praise. People need praise to help them to build their self-confidence and their motivation. Praise should be given on the spot when someone behaves in the way you want them to. There are many ways of giving praise, starting with a simple "Thank you". Giving praise takes no time out of the day of a manager but can have significant benefits.

## Check the Balance

If your team is under-performing and the team members seem poorly motivated, ask yourself how much time you spend giving praise and how much time you spend on disciplinary matters. If you discover that there is an imbalance you'll need to take steps to redress it.

# Case study: Saying "Thank You"

Marina, a small business owner, said that she gave her team consistent and positive feedback. However, the members of her team said that they did not know how they were doing, that they never got feedback, and that they felt unappreciated. Because she was internally motivated Marina was unaware that her staff, who were externally motivated, wanted clear and relevant progress reports and praise. She began to praise her staff when they deserved it. This simple change increased the team's motivation and productivity.

• *Marina's internal motivation had prevented her from realizing that her team members were externally motivated.*
• *By making a small change that cost nothing, she produced good business benefits.*

**Show Appreciation** Even a small gesture, like remembering people's birthdays, will make them feel appreciated for themselves and not just the job they do.

## Clear Your Mind

There are many wrong beliefs about giving praise:

- If they think they're doing well they'll slack.
- If they think the business is doing too well, they'll get complacent.
- To keep them motivated we need to keep them on their toes.

While fear may motivate in specific instances in the short term, holding these kinds of beliefs in the long term is counterproductive to producing sustainable levels of motivation. Managing by fear and criticism will promote distrust, pent-up aggression, disloyalty, lack of team spirit, divisiveness, and lack of responsibility.

## Optimize Feedback

**Positive Intention**
It must have positive intention and be non-judgmental

**Consistent and Fair**
It needs to be perceived as consistent and fair

**Observed and Objective**
It should be comment on observed behaviours, not subjective opinion

**Positive and Developmental**
It should tell people what to do rather than what not to do

# Summary: Learning to Listen

If you are to motivate people effectively, you need to learn to listen to them properly, focusing your full attention on what they are saying. Coaching is an important tool that can enable you to discover what is going on inside people's heads. Phrase your questions properly so that you will get the information you need, and always give good feedback.

## Getting Results by Paying Attention

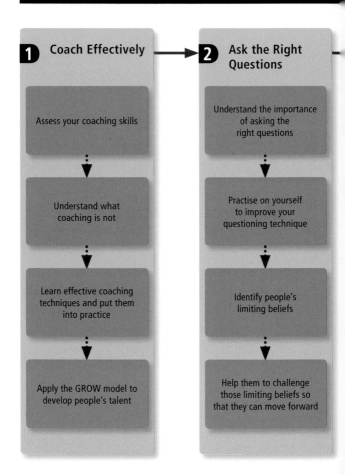

**1 Coach Effectively**

Assess your coaching skills

⋮

Understand what coaching is not

⋮

Learn effective coaching techniques and put them into practice

⋮

Apply the GROW model to develop people's talent

**2 Ask the Right Questions**

Understand the importance of asking the right questions

⋮

Practise on yourself to improve your questioning technique

⋮

Identify people's limiting beliefs

⋮

Help them to challenge those limiting beliefs so that they can move forward

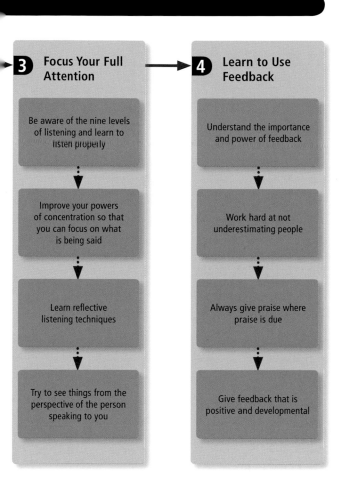

**3** Focus Your Full Attention

→ **4** Learn to Use Feedback

Be aware of the nine levels of listening and learn to listen properly

Improve your powers of concentration so that you can focus on what is being said

Learn reflective listening techniques

Try to see things from the perspective of the person speaking to you

Understand the importance and power of feedback

Work hard at not underestimating people

Always give praise where praise is due

Give feedback that is positive and developmental

# 5

# Sustain Motivation

Knowing your team well is key to sustainable motivation. There are many techniques and skills for finding out more about the people you are working with. This chapter reveals several powerful and effective techniques that are quick and easy to implement. You will be able to discover:

- How to see things from other perspectives
- Why some people are motivated by what they want and why others are motivated by what they don't want
- How to associate yourself with success and dissociate yourself from failure
- How time interpretation affects motivation
- How to build positive associations to access your motivation.

# Build Rapport

To improve as a motivator you need to be aware of all of the messages that you are sending out, not just the verbal ones. Sometimes the subconscious message is conveyed more strongly than the conscious, verbal one.

## Control Non-Verbal Communications

When you walk into an office you can discern almost instantly what the levels of motivation are. This is because a large part of communication is contained not in what is said but in the non-verbal messages that are conveyed. Non-verbal communications include body language, gestures, and voice tonality. You need to be fully aware of the messages that you convey and tune yourself in to the non-spoken messages of your team. For most of us, what we do from moment to moment is one of our unconscious habits. Sometimes our non-verbal communications support us, at other times they don't.

You can create better rapport with others by tuning yourself into non-verbal communications and subtly matching and mirroring elements of people's behaviour.

## Case study: Watching What You're Doing

Sales manager Pedro had a small team of sales and administrative staff and a very large workload, so he felt constantly under pressure. He spent a considerable amount of time out of the office dealing with clients but when he returned to the office his team could read his mood instantly and this would have a negative impact on morale and productivity. Pedro began to pay attention to the negative effect he was having on his team. He learned to bring his feelings under control before he came into the office by using breathing techniques and visualization exercises.

• By paying more attention to his physical state Pedro was able to reduce his team's apprehensions about his mood.
• As a result, his team became more motivated and more productive, which helped to reduce Pedro's workload.

# Learn to Read Non-Verbal Communication

When you master non-verbal communication you will get better results from your team. Tune yourself in to the subtle messages people send through their body language. Are movements expansive or controlled, postures open or closed, breathing deep or shallow, facial expressions upbeat or more severe? Paying attention to such details will prove effective when building rapport with others.

### Note Posture
Take more notice of people's posture, but don't make assumptions. There is a belief that crossed arms means that someone is "closed", yet she might simply be feeling cold or feel comfortable in that position.

### Read Gestures
Pace any consistent use of body movements such as scratching the nose, and pay attention to gestures that you can match subtly, such as crossed legs. Check out the angle at which people sit or stand.

### Reflect the Speaker
Listen carefully to the voice tone and pitch of the person speaking. Match the voice but not to an excessive extent. Listen carefully for key phrases and then repeat them when you are giving your feedback.

# Know How People Communicate

**Everybody's experience of the world is different. This is because it is based on internal representation and will depend upon communication styles. Understanding these styles is important when motivating others.**

## See It, Feel It, Hear It

Think about something you did last week. As you think about it become aware of how you remember it – do you recall images or sounds, or is your memory mainly of how you felt? We experience the world through our five senses of sight, sound, touch, taste, and smell. The three senses people generally pay most attention to are visual (sight), auditory (sound), and kinaesthetic (touch), but we all give different amounts of attention to the different senses at different times. Understanding which senses people are paying most attention to will help you to understand their experience and, therefore, to motivate them better.

**Our senses play a big part in how we communicate**

## Recognize the Type

It is important to recognize whether individuals are primarily visual, auditory, or kinaesthetic so that you can plan some strategies for engaging them.

- **Visual people** will often stand or sit upright or forward with their hands and their bodies erect and their eyes directed upwards. They tend to be organized, neat, well groomed, and orderly. Appearance may be important to them. They memorize by seeing pictures and are not very distracted by noise. They often have difficulty remembering verbal instructions. Words and phrases they might use include "I see", "bright", "colour", "keep an eye out", "eye to eye", "bird's-eye view". They respond well to pictures, videos, diagrams, and graphs. They like to see things from your point of view.

- **Auditory people** are good with verbal instructions and learn by listening. They often like music and enjoy talking on the phone. They like to be told how they're doing and will hear the emotion behind any communication. They are easily distracted by noise. Words and phrases they might use include "hear", "sound", "an earful", "lend me an ear", "listen up", "rings true", "sound as a bell". Tell them stories and make sure you sound good to them. Remember that they will hear any incongruity or lack of enthusiasm in your tone of voice. Use plenty of auditory language.
- **Kinaesthetic people** will often move and talk slowly. They like physical rewards and touching. They memorize by doing. They like to know that something "feels" right. They may well use phrases like "feels fine to me", "get a grip", "hang on". In a meeting you need to let them have hands-on experiences. How they feel, about you and about themselves, is very important. Use stories to evoke the emotional states you want.

**Read the Signs** People's pastimes and interests will often give you a clue as to their communication styles, enabling you to engage with them meaningfully.

# Walk a Mile in Their Shoes

**Being able to switch perceptions, to understand something from someone else's point of view, is an essential motivation skill. Motivated people usually have a greater understanding of the behaviours of others.**

## Switch Positions

Less motivated people often lack the ability to step into another's shoes and become stuck in unresourceful situations. Being able to "switch" positions is a useful strategy when motivating others. There are three perceptual positions – first, second, and third.

- **First position** – When you see something from your own point of view. It's your take on the situation. Many people spend most of their time in first position. Comments such as, "He just does not see my point of view" would suggest someone stuck in this position. First position is useful for understanding what is important to you. If you always put others first, spending more time in first position is critical for you.
- **Second position** – When you see things from someone else's point of view. Some people rarely experience true second position! As a motivator second position will help you to understand the person you are trying to motivate. As all motivation comes from inside, without this capability you will always be limited as a motivator.
- **Third position** – An objective "fly on the wall" view. You can see and hear the individuals involved but you cannot experience their feelings.

> You'll see more from a new perspective

**There are no impossible dreams, just our limited perception of what is possible.**

Beth Mende Conny

## Adopt Different Positions

**Learning how to adopt different positions is a powerful motivation and life tool and one that it is well worth spending time on. It is a strategy that will enable you to deal with challenges and frustrations more resourcefully.**

If there are times when you don't understand the behaviour of others or feel frustrated by their actions, it will help to look at your reaction from different perspectives.

### Reframe Events

An event that often affects motivation is a complaint from a customer. Take yourself through this exercise by thinking of a time when you felt annoyed by a customer's complaint, paying attention to your reactions to the event.

| Position | Focus |
|---|---|
| You're in first position, having just received a customer's complaint. | What do you see, hear, and feel in first position? What is important to you here? How are you approaching this situation? |
| Break your state and imagine yourself in second position, "the shoes" of the customer. | What does he see, hear, and feel in this situation? What is important to him? How does he think he is approaching this situation? |
| Break your state and put yourself into third position, that of an uninvolved bystander. | What do you see and hear? How do you think these two people (first and second) are interacting? What do you think about the interaction/situation? |
| Break your state again and imagine that you are a consultant with all of the information from all three parties. | What advice would you give to yourself? What do you need to learn from this situation? How can you improve this situation? What do you think you could do to create a win-win scenario here? |

# Use Motivational Filters

**The brain filters the information it receives so that it can select what is most important. Understanding how personal filters work can help you to motivate people in the most appropriate way.**

## Judge the Importance of Information

Information is filtered through experiences, values, beliefs, and attitudes. Two of the most useful filter patterns are known as the internal/external filter and the towards/away from filter. If you can identify which filter is operating when you are dealing with people you will have a better idea of what will motivate them.

- **Internal/External Filter** The internal/external filter determines how people know something is true. Internal people will use their own references and experiences to make the decision internally, whereas external people will look for corroboration from someone or something external to themselves. How do you know when you've done a good job at work? Is it because you know or is it because someone tells you?

## Speak the Right Language

You will need to know someone's motivational direction if you are going to use the right language when speaking to him. Consider the impact of these two statements:

→ When you achieve your goals this month you will be first in line for promotion.

→ You must achieve your targets this month or we will not be able to promote you.

The first statement will be more of a driver if the person you are speaking to is *towards* motivated whereas the second will be more motivational if he is *away from* motivated.

- **Towards/Away From** This
filter operates when people
are motivated either by moving
towards what they want or
moving away from what they

**Identify the Motivator**
Unlike adults children do
not let comparison and
embarrassment affect
their motivation levels.

don't want. Think about why you go to work in the
morning. What's your motivation? Do you jump out of
bed thinking about what you can achieve today or do
you get up on time to avoid being late for work?

## Tailor Feedback to the Individual

When giving feedback to your team members it is
important to know whether they are internally or
externally motivated. Feedback given in the wrong way
may well not be "heard" by the employee. Some people
just know that they've done a good job (internal), whereas
others need to be told, thanked, or rewarded (external).
Many senior managers are internally motivated and do
not need anyone else to tell them when they have done
a good job. Because of this they may not feel the need to
tell others when they have done a good job. This could
result in an externally motivated team member feeling
demotivated and unappreciated.

# Consider Motivational Factors

**How you feel about any experience is determined by the meaning that you attach to it. Learning to reframe your experience will help you to interpret events positively.**

## Giving Meaning to Events

All events are neutral, it is people who give them meaning. It is possible to reframe experiences and attach a more positive meaning to any situation.

- One person may be devastated that he did not get promoted whereas another may be happy that he didn't.
- Their reactions depend totally upon the meaning that each attaches to the situation.
- The first individual may be focused on the pain of missing out or on lost income, whereas the second may be thinking that it means that he can spend more time with his friends and family.

**5 minute FIX**

Think about a situation that is causing you concern. Ask yourself:

- What meaning do I currently attach to this situation/event?
- What could be good about this situation?
- How can I turn this situation around?
- What can I learn from this situation?
- What other meanings could be attached to this situation?

## Learn to Reframe Experiences

As a motivator it is important that you learn how to ask the questions that will help people to consider their reaction to an event and to reframe themselves by changing their negative reactions. Common situations that will require reframing when working to motivate others include problems with commuting to work, failure to achieve targets, problems with colleagues, receiving negative feedback from clients or a manager. Be aware of how you interpret situations that affect you. As a successful motivator you may be a role model for your team, so ensure that you interpret situations positively.

## Reframe Events

Look at these examples of common events and note how they can be interpreted in different ways by different people in different circumstances. Think about frequently occurring events that could be interpreted negatively by members of your team. Think about how you can help them to reframe their experiences and see their situation in a more positive light.

| Event | Negative Meaning | Reframe |
|-------|-----------------|---------|
| Complaints from clients | No one appreciates us. We're always messing up. We'll probably lose the client now. | This is an opportunity to reconnect with the client and provide an even better service. |
| Being stuck in traffic | I'm going to be late, I'll be in trouble, and I am going to get behind with my work. | I can use the time out to plan the rest of my week. |
| Feedback from your manager | He always criticizes me. He thinks I am useless. | Feedback is the food of champions. He wants to help me to improve. |
| Losing a deal | It always happens to me. I'll never manage to hit my targets now. | Every lost deal takes me one step closer to a deal. I can learn from this experience and improve next time. |
| Attending training | It's a waste of my time. It won't be relevant. I could be doing something more useful. | I could learn something that will help me. It's good that my organization values me. |
| Paperwork/ administration | It's a complete waste of my valuable time. It's unnecessary and it's beneath me. | Everyone has to do it. It's essential. It's good to get things finished. |

**TIP** **When one of your team expresses an opinion with a negative meaning attached, reframe him by asking, "Are you absolutely sure that's true? "**

# Get Associated with Success

**How you remember past events affects your emotions and will play a significant part in your day-to-day motivation levels. Learn to associate with positive experiences and dissociate from negative ones.**

## Recognize your State

Think of a recent conversation with a friend. As you remember it, are you living in the experience as if it is happening now (associated state) or are you experiencing it as if you are outside your own body (dissociated state)?

- In an associated state you experience past events as if they are happening now. You see what you saw, hear what you heard, and feel what you felt. Association is good for reliving positive experiences and recalling resourceful emotions. Anchoring and goal setting are more effective when the associated state is utilized.

- In a dissociated state you are an observer of events. Dissociation is useful when taking feedback, when dealing with criticism, or when coping with a painful or traumatic situation.

**Associate with the Good Times**
When you access your happy, fun-filled memories you can increase your motivation by connecting with all of the positive emotions that you experienced during those times.

## Become Aware of Your State

Generally people fit into one of four categories. By becoming more aware of your habitual state you can access other states to enrich the quality of your experience.

- Associated to all experiences – you experience huge highs and lows as you associate fully into both positive and negative experiences.
- Dissociating from all experiences – you can distance yourself from difficult situations and choices but you may never really experience the full range of positive emotions within any situation.
- Dissociation from positive and association into negative – you may be unhappy, as you can fully relive and re-experience negative emotions but are never able to connect completely with your positive experiences.
- Association into positive and dissociation from negative – you can relive positive experiences and choose to step back from negative experiences, allowing you to be more objective and less emotional about them.

> **Sow a habit and you reap a character; sow a character and you reap a destiny.**
>
> Ralph Waldo Emerson

# Use Imagery to Boost Motivation

Your internal image of an experience or a future event will determine how you feel about it. By using imagery to "improve" the experience you can alter the emotions produced by the event to motivate yourself effectively.

## Notice Different Elements

Changing the characteristics or qualities of an experience will change the quality of that experience significantly. By learning how to change these characteristics you can effectively programme your mind to make you feel more motivated to do things that you wouldn't usually want to do. Think about two tasks that you had to perform. You enjoy one of the tasks and felt motivated to do it, but the other one holds no appeal for you and you procrastinated until you had no choice but to do it. In each case, the characteristics of the experience of performing the task will have been very different. If you can "improve" these factors you will be able to change your internal coding of the experience and how it makes you feel.

## TECHNIQUES *to* practise

Think of a time when you felt totally motivated. By experimenting with different elements of this image you will change the intensity of the feelings. Try the following and see what works best for you.

- Are you in the picture? Step into it and experience it as if you are in it.
- What size is the picture? Increase it until it is life-sized.

- Do you see the picture in black and white or in colour? See the picture in vivid colour.
- Is the sound low or high? Turn up the volume.
- How bright is the picture? Increase the brightness of the picture until the image is brightly lit.
- Is it a still photograph or a movie? Add movement and life to the image until it becomes real for you.

# Case study: Changing Your Experience

Melanie, a sales executive, was competent in all areas of her work except when presenting sales solutions to clients. She was capable when practising but would become nervous and worried when making the presentation in front of a "live" client. After working with her sales coach on changing her mental pictures of past and future events, Melanie was able to make her presentations more confidently and more successfully.

• *Prior to her coaching sessions Melanie was forming more powerful negative images than positive ones.*
• *She was able to increase her confidence by improving her positive visualizations.*
• *By seeing herself presenting confidently and successfully Melanie was soon able to improve her sales results.*

## Be Present

As you think about your goal do you see yourself doing the task (dissociated) or are you actually experiencing yourself doing it (associated)? This distinction can make a huge difference to the levels of emotion that you attach to an experience. If you can imagine yourself experiencing the event it will be more powerful. Focusing on the results you want and the benefits that you gain from them in this way helps to stimulate your mind and acts as a motivator. This clarity of vision also serves to create a positive mental state and an anticipation of success. You can use these positive emotions to drive the necessary short-term activities that are required. As you focus on your outcomes in this way your mind will also begin to notice resources and opportunities that will help you to achieve your goals. These resources were always there, but your brain did not recognize them until achieving your objectives became a reality.

**TIP** To remove negative associations from events, dissociate yourself fully.

# How Time Affects Motivation

Why are some people always late while others are on time? Why are some people always on top of their projects while others rush to finish? The relationship with time is a significant motivational factor.

## Different Views of Time

There are those who live in the moment ("in time" people) and are not that aware of time passing, and those who are much more aware of time and who plan and organize ("through time" people). Awareness of the personalities and characteristics of these two types is essential for the professional motivator. Personal coding of time affects behaviours when it comes to dealing with difficult scenarios, running meetings, organizing projects, making decisions, setting goals, and meeting targets.

## Recognize In Time People

In time people live for the moment. When you work with them in a meeting or on a project they are "fully present" and are not easily distracted. They have a tendency to mistake the time, will often be late, and may have difficulty finishing meetings and phone calls. They like to keep their options open and are not usually good planners.

## think
### SMART

**People at either extreme of the time spectrum can sometimes create problems in an organization and you need to assess their situation carefully.**

It may not be wise to give a very in time person responsibility for managing a project with many small checklists or asking a through time person to deliver a presentation without giving him a timescale and checkpoints. Ensure that you adapt your management approach to get the best out of the person whom you are managing.

## Which Time Type Are You?

It's quite easy to establish which approach you have to time. Read these statements and choose which statements you agree with.

| In Time | Through Time |
|---|---|
| You are often surprised by the amount of time that has passed since you last noticed what time it was. | You usually have a good idea of what time it is. |
| You like to decide in the moment, keeping your options open. | You plan and prepare, making decisions in advance. |
| You are often late. | You're usually on time. |
| You are constantly rushing to meet last-minute deadlines. | Your know what your deadlines are and plan to meet them. |
| You often get talking when you have something to do. | You end conversations to get on with the task in hand. |
| Your diary is a mess/you have no diary. | Your diary is well organized. |
| You'll see what happens and go with the flow. | You plan your days on paper or in your head and then work out your plan. |

## Recognize Through Time People

Through time people are much more aware of time. They plan their movements and actions and will often use planning tools such as diaries and schedules. They are often frustrated by in time people and may regard them as disorganized. They will usually be on time for their appointments and will have no problem bringing meetings to a close when the allotted time is up. Disorganized environments can distract them. In time people will frequently find that through time people are slightly clinical in their approach to time.

**TIP** **Think about whether your team members are in time or through time people and how you can use this information to help them to achieve more.**

# Anchor Positive States

**Have you ever heard a piece of music and been reminded of a particular event? Naturally occurring anchors link a specific mental state with an external trigger or stimulus such as a smell, a sound, or a place.**

## Break Negative Responses

Potentially negative anchors will already be in place within your workplace and you need to work to remove them and replace them with new, positive ones. Common areas for negative responses include group meetings, targets, closed-door meetings, managerial behaviours, and poorly phrased e-mails. It is easy to replace most negative responses with positive ones – it usually just needs a little thought and a few modifications of the behaviours that are producing the negative anchors.

## Replacing Negative Anchors

When meetings are unproductive and staff seem uninterested in the content and outcome of the meetings, it may be possible to improve performance by taking a few simple steps to break the pattern and replace their negative responses by:

→ Varying the times and locations of the meetings
→ Changing the seating arrangement
→ Altering the content and format of the meetings
→ Getting the staff more involved
→ Bringing in a guest speaker
→ Being more energetic.

Keep the meetings focused on positive results and constructive development. When you move all problem-focused issues outside the meeting you will discover that you can establish new, positive associations, and your meetings will soon become a celebration of energy, enthusiasm, and creativity.

## Ivan Pavlov's Experiment

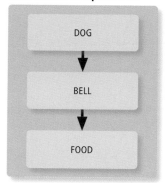

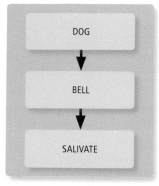

**A Conditioned Response** Pavlov experimented with dogs by ringing a bell each time they were fed. The dogs began to link the bell with being fed.

Eventually, just ringing the bell caused the dogs to salivate in anticipation of receiving food. The dogs were merely reacting to the stimulus.

## Build Positive Anchors

Being able to build new positive anchors that you can use to motivate yourself or others at any time is an effective management tool.

- Remember a time when you felt totally motivated and completely in control.
- Choose a word, an image, and a physical gesture that sum those feelings up.
- As you relive that time repeat the word to yourself, see the image, and physically make the gesture.
- Practise getting into those good feelings until they are associated with the word, the image, and the gesture.
- You will be able to access them any time you need them just by using the word, the image, or the gesture.

You may become so good at accessing your positive anchors in any situation that you will automatically dismiss the negative feelings associated with an event and react positively to the things that happen to you.

**TIP** The more intense the emotion that you link to, the more powerful the trigger will become.

# Summary: The Motivational Edge

To be a really good motivator you will need to learn to harness the inspiration and energy of the great motivators. Find out what motivates others by building a rapport with them, stepping into their shoes to understand what they are feeling. In order to achieve success in your own life, learn to associate with success.

## Staying Motivated

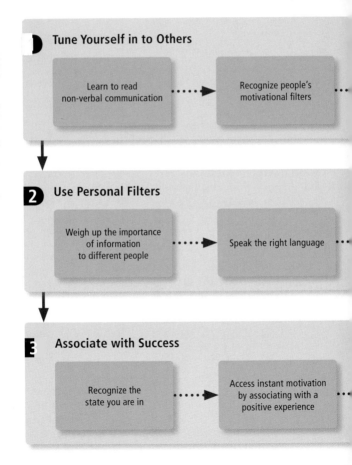

**Tune Yourself in to Others**

Learn to read non-verbal communication ·····▶ Recognize people's motivational filters ···

**2** **Use Personal Filters**

Weigh up the importance of information to different people ·····▶ Speak the right language ···

**3** **Associate with Success**

Recognize the state you are in ·····▶ Access instant motivation by associating with a positive experience ···

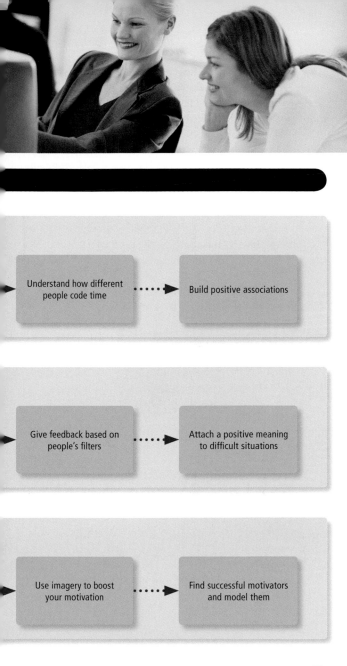

| Understand how different people code time | ┈┈┈▶ | Build positive associations |

| Give feedback based on people's filters | ┈┈┈▶ | Attach a positive meaning to difficult situations |

| Use imagery to boost your motivation | ┈┈┈▶ | Find successful motivators and model them |

# Model Peak Performance

Great motivators know how to harness the inspiration and energy of the most motivated people in the world. One of the best ways to learn how to motivate is to identify a great motivator and model his strategies.

## Model Improved Motivational Skills

Modelling is useful for capturing the success of others and making it your own, breaking out of your comfort zone, thinking creatively, acquiring new skills, learning and developing strategies, and getting motivated. Modelling well is an essential success skill and the more time you spend perfecting it, the more powerful a tool it will become for you. You need to focus on skills, behaviours, and shadowing rather than on conscious rationalization. Children learn at a phenomenal rate because of their insatiable curiosity and their lack of limitation.

## TECHNIQUES *to* practise

**If you need to acquire a skill or strategy to deal with a specific situation, select as your role model someone you know who has the beliefs and values that are appropriate to your situation.**

- Watch your model do the task you need to do. Pay attention to what he does and says and how he interacts with others and their environment. Pay attention to detail and the process he uses.

- Ask questions that help you to understand why your role model does what he does. "Why did you do that? What were you thinking when you did that? What do you believe about...?"

- Act as if you are your role model and try out the task for yourself so that you know how it feels from his perspective.

- Refine the core components of the task and carry on asking questions until you are able to do the task effectively.

# Case study: Trying a New Approach

Lauren, a young sales director, had recently been given some stiff sales quotas. With a new, unproven, and demotivated team she was currently not even meeting her existing targets. Lauren knew that her beliefs, attitudes, and behaviours were not supporting her but she did not know what to do. After spending some time with a sales director who had encountered similar challenges, she was able to make changes that helped her to remotivate the team.

• *Lauren knew that if other people were getting results in similar circumstances they would have strategies that could help her to meet her targets.*
• *She spent time uncovering, understanding, and implementing the correct strategies.*
• *She was open enough to take on board feedback and try a new approach that enabled her to meet her targets and motivate her team to work with her.*

## Identify Your Role Models

Top performers believe that if one person can do it, so can you. Think about people who could be your role models. You can select different role models for different skills, strategies, and situations. Your role models do not have to be people you know – you can model people through books, the Internet, and television.

## Spend Time with Your Model

Ideally, however, your role model should be someone with whom you can spend some time as he works. Choose someone whose skill makes him a model of excellence. Assess this excellence by comparing your model to others working in the same field, and by looking for signs of his effortless achievement and mastery. You are more likely to succeed if you aim your aspirations as high as possible.

---

**TIP** When faced with a challenging situation ask yourself, "What would (your role model) do?"

---

# Index

## Picture Credits

The publisher would like to thank the following for their kind permission to reproduce their photographs: Abbreviations key : (l) = left, (c) = centre, (r) = right, (t) = top, (b) = below, (cl) = centre left, (cr) = centre right.

**1:** Tony Metaxas/Asia Images/Getty (l), Meeke/zefa/Corbis (c), Randy Faris/Corbis (r); **2:** BanaStock/PunchStock/JupiterImages; **3:** Wide Group/Iconica/Getty (t), Chabruken/Taxi/Getty (c), Seth Joel/Photographer's Choice/Getty (b); **5:** Wide Group/Iconica/Getty; **7:** Liquidlibrary/Alamy; **8:** Marc Romanelli/The Image Bank/Getty (l), M. Thomsen/zefa/Corbis (cl), Ashok Charles/Taxi/Getty (cr), Wide Group/Iconica/Getty (r); **13:** Euan Myles/Stone/Getty; **14:** Meeke/zefa/Corbis; **21:** Marc Romanelli/The Image Bank/Getty; **26:** Logan Mock-Bunting/Reportage/Getty; **29:** PunchStock; **31:** Chabruken/Taxi/Getty; **33:** Steven Puetzer/Photonica/Getty; **42:** Zia Soleil/Iconica/Getty (tl), Michael Krasowitz/Taxi/Getty (bl), PunchStock (br); **47:** M. Thomsen/zefa/Corbis; **51:** Chabruken/Taxi/Getty; **53:** Grove Pashley/Photis/JupiterImages; **56:** Michael Hemsley; **62:** Randy Faris/Corbis; **66:** Simon Marcus/Corbis; **73:** Michael Hemsley; **75:** Charles Maraia/Photonica/Getty; **77:** PM Images/The Image Bank/Getty; **83:** Wide Group/Iconica/Getty; **86:** Seth Joel/Photographer's Choice/Getty; **91:** Wide Group/Iconica/Getty; **93:** Wide Group/Iconica/Getty; **95:** Doug Landreth/Science Faction/Getty; **97:** Chabruken/Taxi/Getty (tl), Yellow Dog Productions/The Image Bank/Getty (tr), PunchStock (b); **99:** Tom Grill/Iconica/Getty; **103:** Ross Whitaker/The Image Bank/Getty; **106:** Ashok Charles/Taxi/Getty; **115:** Johner Images/Getty.

All other images © Dorling Kindersley.

For further information see www.dkimages.com

## Authors' acknowledgments

I'd like to thank all at Dorling Kindersley for their help in completing this book – a true team effort. Special thanks to Adèle Hayward and to Simon Tuite, and to Fiona Biggs for her excellent work. Also, thanks to all those who have supported my journey thus far – you know who you are!

## Authors' biography

As an expert in sales and motivation Gavin Ingham helps people to increase performance by turning self-doubt, fear, and lack of motivation into self-belief, confidence, and action. Gavin is a published author and has recorded numerous sales audio and DVD programmes. His products sell worldwide and his seminars are attended by thousands of people every year. For more details of his programmes and for free resources/newsletters, visit www.gaviningham.net.